NO CURE FOR CANCER

D1115171

NO
CURE
FOR
CANCER

DENIS LEARY

ANCHOR BOOKS DOUBLEDAY

NEW YORK   LONDON   TORONTO   SYDNEY   AUCKLAND

AN ANCHOR BOOK

PUBLISHED BY DOUBLEDAY

a division of Bantam Doubleday Dell Publishing Group, Inc.

666 Fifth Avenue, New York, New York 10103

ANCHOR BOOKS, DOUBLEDAY, and the portrayal of an anchor
are trademarks of Doubleday, a division of Bantam Doubleday
Dell Publishing Group, Inc.

No Cure for Cancer was directed by Chris Phillips

Music and Lyrics by Denis Leary, Chris Phillips and Adam Roth

Lighting and Scenic Design by Larry Lieberman

Sound Design by Peter Klusman

Publicity by Parenteau Guidance and The Glenn Schwartz Co.

Originally produced in the summer of 1990 at the Assembly Ballroom
for the Edinburgh International Arts Festival by Jason M. Solomon
and Jonathon Thoday

Produced in the fall of 1990 at the Bloomsbury Theatre in London by Avalon
Promotions and Jason M. Solomon

Library of Congress Cataloging-in-Publication Data

Leary, Denis.

No cure for cancer. — 1st Anchor Books ed.

p.   cm.

I. Title.

PS3562.E2397N6   1992

812'.54—dc20   92-16820

CIP

BOOK DESIGN BY BONNI LEON

ISBN 0-385-42581-3

Copyright © 1992 by Denis Leary

ALL RIGHTS RESERVED

PRINTED IN THE UNITED STATES OF AMERICA

FIRST ANCHOR BOOKS EDITION: NOVEMBER 1992

10   9   8   7   6   5   4

TO
ANN,
JACK,
DEVIN AND
MY PARENTS
NORA AND JOHN

CONTENTS

ACKNOWLEDGMENTS

I must thank the following people, without whose advice, ammunition and assistance *No Cure for Cancer*—the show and the book—would not have happened:

Kiwi, Blades, Noose, Gronk, Head, Fitzy, Sully, Doug, The Macs, Mike McGinn, Ann Lembeck, George Gilmore, Jim Serpico, C. C. Calloway, Chastity Phillips, Cary Hoffman, James Dixon, Glenn Schwartz, Michael O'Brien, Matt Dillon, Gail Parenteau, Regan Kennedy, Terry Quinn, Adam Roth, Ted Demme, Dan Strone, Chris Young, Alan Kannof, Colin Quinn, Tony V., Babe Ruth, Tony C., Bob Stanley, Joe Foy, Ace Bailey, Jon Stewart, Lise Mayer, Frank Skinner, Pamela Ross, Jason M. Solomon, Chris Phillips, David Baddiel, Jonathon Thoday, Richard Turner, Laurie Zaks, Mike Klinghoffer, Mary Salter, Bob Kreek, Jonathan Ross, Charlie Conrad, Katy Bolger, Dr. James Randall, Steve and Judy Howe, Ann Marie and Betsy.

A NOTE FROM THE DIRECTOR

Working with Denis Leary was the single worst experience of my professional life. I quit. I am leaving the theatre. I am leaving New York. I'm going to open a little wicker craft shop in the mountains and try to forget ever having met this vicious, untalented scum.

—*Chris Phillips*
Winooski, Vermont
September 1992

INTRODUCTION

In March 1990, I flew to London to perform on a BBC television show called "Paramount City." I was accompanied by my wife Ann, who was six months pregnant at the time. We arrived on a Thursday, I was scheduled to tape the show Saturday night and we would fly home on Sunday. A short little weekend overseas. Do some sightseeing, eat some bad English food, complain about the weather, curse the Queen and come home. The typical American's trip abroad. My wife's doctor had okayed the trip. Everything was in order.

Saturday morning, Ann's water broke. We rushed to the hospital in a black cab, where we were ever so politely informed that she was to stay in bed on round-the-clock observation for the next three months—or until the baby was born, whichever came first. We had been in England less than forty-eight hours. I was already beginning to miss New York and hot pastrami and spring training and big cars and air conditioning and drive-by shootings and cable TV. Now we were going to have to settle in. Once Ann was stabilized, I ran off to the Paramount Theatre and my previous engagement.

The taping was a blur, although I vaguely remember someone mentioning the word "riot" backstage. I, of course, assumed they were referring to my performance, a seven-minute set of stand-up comedy. However, when I tried to leave the building, I was stopped by a phalanx of English policemen as a crowd of a few thousand people stormed past, stopping only to turn over a green Jaguar and set it ablaze. I was in the middle of the Poll Tax Riot —some thirty thousand protesters rebelling against Margaret Thatcher's government by burning and beating and looting and leering. It was three hours before I was allowed to leave the theatre, and another on foot before I got back to the hospital.

The point of all this is to explain how *No Cure for Cancer* came to be. Due to my wife's hospitalization and the resulting extension of our weekend trip, we were around the following Monday to read the good reviews my performance on "Paramount City" received. The producers asked me back the following weekend. That performance got even more attention.

My son Jack was born two days later—twelve weeks ahead of schedule. He was placed in intensive care and the doctors informed us that he would not be able to fly home for another five months.

While stuck in England, I met a very funny writer and comedian named David Baddiel, who introduced me to his manager, Jon Thoday. Jon had seen me on TV and suggested that, since I was in the U.K. for the duration, I should think about performing at the Edinburgh International Arts Festival, the oldest performing arts festival in the world. For three weeks every August dancers, actors, musicians, painters, alcoholics, drug addicts, filmmakers and the French converge in Scotland and ply their wares. Jon shot off an impressive list of those who had appeared there: Bogosian, Cleese, Olivier, Cook, Moore, Sellers, Huston. And he encouraged me to put together a one-man show that he would produce. That's when the whole thing clicked. I had nothing but time on my hands—no cable, no baseball, no gigs lined up. For years I had been telling myself I wanted to do a one-man show, and now the opportunity not only presented itself —it rammed itself right down my throat.

I had tried the stand-up comedy circuit but never found it very satisfying. As an undergraduate at Emerson College in Boston, I had studied acting and writing, but acting parts were hard to come by for first- and second-year students since upper classmen had performance credits to fulfill. Those of us interested in acting needed an outlet and fortunately the Comedy Workshop, under the auspices of Emerson professor James Randall, provided it. Jim had been a blessing during my undergraduate years. He had helped to push the school to recognize and payroll the Workshop, which gave us creative freedom to write and perform everything from theatrical sketches to original one- and two-act plays, short films and video pieces. After graduation I had stayed on to teach in the Workshop, a job I much preferred to my other part-time jobs as a delivery driver and janitor and hotel switchboard operator and pourer of sulfuric acid into jars at a mixing plant on the Boston waterfront.

Yet I was soon frustrated. The classroom work with actors and writers was making me hungry to put something onstage. But if parts are hard to find in New York and L.A., in Boston they're virtually nonexistent. I did some work at the Charles Playhouse (one of those "yeah, you got the part—by the way, can you also paint scenery and sell tickets and clean the toilet?" theatrical experiences), but that was about it.

Several of my Emerson classmates were working as stand-up comics. The money was minuscule then, but they were getting onstage for ten to fifteen minutes five or six times a week. I got up the nerve and signed the call sheet one night. It was one of the worst experiences of my life. I had written a piece about drugs or drinking or death, I can't remember the subject matter, but I do remember that it required me to roll around on the stage writhing and moaning. At one point I looked up and saw rows of puzzled-looking people staring down at me.

I remember their silence. I remember the emcee pointing to his watch and waving frantically at me. I remember sweating and thinking how remarkable it was that I was soaking wet on the outside but had not one drop of moisture in my mouth. I remember standing backstage, frozen against a wall, for about an hour. I can't remember ever feeling that bad about anything.

So, of course, I went back for more the next night, and night after night after that—screaming and ranting and rolling and sweating. Eventually—very eventually—I got a laugh.

I became a regular at the comedy clubs and occasionally got the odd paid set. Boston comics like Don Gavin, Steve Sweeney or Lenny Clarke would give me ten minutes in one of their headlining shows. They didn't care if I sucked. They'd been there themselves. They knew that stand-up comedy is an acting class that takes place onstage in front of a live audience, that you cannot learn the skill unless you're on your feet in front of a sea of faces waiting for the next thought to pop into your head and out of your mouth. That's what I love about stand-up —the rush of making it happen now, *right now*. Immediate action. Immediate response.

Unfortunately, due to my teaching responsibilities and my part-time jobs, comedy became almost a sideline, a hobby, and that was a mistake. After a few months my performing muscles got flabby. Because I was paying the rent and putting food on the table through other work, I didn't get desperate about stage time. But I also realized that if I wanted to develop as a comic and actor I needed to have nothing else on the horizon. Total commitment. Hunger. A bunker mentality. So I quit teaching, quit my part-time jobs and moved into an apartment that was basically a bunker with a sink.

I quit simply feeling around in a box for what might be funny and began to dredge up humor from my own experience. My sense of humor and outlook had always been marked by a black streak; therefore the material I came up with was dark. Very dark. But it was the kind of material I'd always had on my mind.

Suddenly, I'd found my voice.

When I began to try out this new material in comedy clubs I got a few laughs but often the audiences did not like what I had to say. In the late eighties, comedy was big business. The clubs were bigger than ever and they were everywhere. And as a result the product was becoming watered down. Club owners wanted to book safe performers who would please the most people. No risk, no rummy. It was like disco all over again. Certain clubs in certain cities still had the kind of crowd that would follow you anywhere. Even if they weren't laughing, they were waiting and watching. But overall, I got people who walked out or protested that "there are just some things you shouldn't laugh at."

After a while I got tired of defending myself. I can't

explain my sense of humor or my world view. I was born in Worcester, Massachusetts—a dank, polluted, angst-ridden city filled with factories and friction. Birthplace of Abbie Hoffman. Heroin capital of the East Coast. I'm Irish. I'm Catholic. I'm guilty as charged. My first childhood memory begins at twelve thirty-five on Friday, November 22, 1963, and ends three days later—after a shooting, a wake, a funeral and another shooting. I don't blame my parents or society or even myself. I blame Jack Ruby. Every single weekend since has been a huge disappointment.

Once I decided to dwell on the demons in my psyche and let them roam about the stage there was no going back. Even on nights when whole chunks of the audience would get hostile or walk away, the thrill of being truthful to the moment—of dealing head on with my own fears and obsessions—was exhilarating. Death, disease, hypocrisy, political correctness, drugs, drink, smoking and all the other subjects I had found funny were now my normal target. Comedy has always seemed to me to be about bursting the bubble of pretension, breaking the rules. The stage is built for free speech on speed and, once someone gets a little too tall, I like to knock them down a few notches. Some audiences didn't find my routine funny. Neither did some club owners. I did.

You can only work so long in front of the irked and the untouchable, the protesting and the prude. I decided to forgo the lucrative comedy circuit, where the directive "Don't say *fuck*" is just the tip of a common agenda that means "Make fun of homosexuality, women and Dan Quayle." Where developing an edgy approach means not wearing a tie. It's comedy-by-numbers, the equivalent of the dogs-playing-poker paintings that Elvis loved so much. Elvis would have hated my act.

My friend Tony V. gave me a regular slot on his weekly show at the Charles Playhouse. Whenever I had doubts about the direction I was headed, Tony was there to urge me on with his all-encompassing motto: "They all suck." He and his wife Kristen Johnson got me involved in production at the Charlestown Working Theater and the Boston Shakespeare Company's New Voices Workshop.

I spent a year doing my own show one night a week in Boston at a place called Sam's. The owner was a big, burly Irishman named Maloney who hated my guts and later died after doctors found a tumor the size of Nell Carter behind his right ear. But the booking agent was a guy named Barry Katz who told me, "Do whatever you want—just don't break anything." This basically amounted to two hours of stage time every Thursday night when I could say *what* I wanted *how* I wanted. I had found my audience. They were roughly my age. They wanted something different. There were about twenty-five of them.

No matter, though, because my act was gaining momentum. I moved to New York and started working late night sets in the downtown clubs. It was mostly preaching to the converted—after-hours people on the prowl for something dark. Out-of-work actors, addled insomniacs, lone drinkers, bass players. The dirt. The dregs. The people who at two in the morning wanted to see you push your luck as far as it would go. To test your nerves and theirs.

An Emerson classmate of mine, Eddie Brill, was running his own club in the Village and he let me go onstage at odd hours to rant and rave. I got mentioned in a *New York Post* piece. It said, "Denis Leary spread eight seconds of material over what seemed like forty-five days."

We laughed. We cried. We drank a bottle of tequila. We bought an Uzi and tried to find out where the critic lived.

In spite of the *Post*, I knew I was on the right track. Hoy Boy, an old friend, was mounting a show called "The Blue Light Club" downtown at the Acme. A group of fifteen actors and musicians would improvise a new show from an outline each week. He gave me a slot and total creative freedom. We did it once a week for eight months. We laughed. We cried. We drank bottles of Robitussin and fell asleep.

I was getting the itch to develop a long piece, to take even bigger bites, to dive down deep into the pond and filch from the bottom. Somewhere between Eric Bogosian's on-the-edge character monologues and Spalding Gray's finely detailed reminiscence, I thought there was room for something that combined elements of both. A first-person piece that went over the edge.

Jon Thoday's Edinburgh offer couldn't have come at a better time. I would have three and a half months to write and prepare a show before previews and another week before it opened.

I began with the material I'd honed in Boston and New York. Combining that with a few older pieces, some new notes and improvisational segments, I polished various parts of the show in London clubs, standing onstage and emptying my head of whatever thoughts I had on a particular subject. Sometimes the subjects were general, like death. Sometimes they were specific, like Elvis's death.

I didn't script these performances. Instead I would rush offstage and make feverish notes as the material took shape. Chris Phillips, another Emerson classmate, flew to England and we spent hours hammering at the ideas, adding music and fine-tuning my stage routine. My wife Ann deserves recognition for her constant encouragement and support during this time, as well as for her detailed suggestions that helped shape the show.

No Cure for Cancer previewed to very favorable reviews at the Croydon Art Center in London in late July 1990. We tinkered with it a bit and debuted at the Assembly Ballroom Theatre in Edinburgh ten days later. The reviews were terrific. The run was sold out by the morning of the second day. The show won the Critics Award and the BBC Festival Recommendation. There were some protests about the title, but I found it the perfect metaphor for society in general and my generation in particular. We snorted and drank and rocked our way through the last twenty years and now—sobered and surprised—we wonder why the problems on the planet haven't been fixed. Fuck us and the polyester flares we rode in on.

The original version contained an opening monologue performed by Dave Baddiel. In November we moved to the Bloomsbury Theatre in London's West End. Adam Roth joined Chris on guitar as we added more music to the top of the show. British performance artist Simon Parker performed the opening monologue.

We brought the show to New York in October 1991 and producer Jason Solomon had some vital suggestions —dropping the opening monologue and adding more music toward the end. Adam and I essentially wrote the final song onstage one night, as he improvised a chord progression and I let fly with a dark dive on the mortality theme. It worked. Lise Mayer, a fine British writer with a wealth of experience, flew over and spent three weeks, offering invaluable criticism. Chris and I also developed additional material under the outlined themes, resulting in over thirty new minutes in the New York show.

It served us well. We laughed. We cried. We ran naked

through the park. We rubbed each other down with fistfuls of Mineral Ice and sang at the moon. Well, not really. I wouldn't call it singing. It was more like a howl.

The version of *No Cure for Cancer* that appears here was transcribed from several shows and includes stage directions to orient the reader and to guide the intrepid performer.

There's the setup.

Now here's the punch line: my son Jack not only lived, he prospered. He now weighs about thirty pounds and can throw a tablespoon over twenty-five feet.

D.L.
New York City
April 1992

"Write what you know, kid."

       —Jesus to the Apostle Paul, A.D. 33

No Cure for Cancer was originally produced for the New York stage by Jason M. Solomon and Pamela Ross in association with Comedy Central at the Actors' Playhouse, Greenwich Village, on October 23, 1991.

(Iggy Pop's "Lust For Life" plays in house. The stage is dark. As the song fades out, the loud jangling chords of another song take over. The stage slowly comes to light, revealing deep velvet drapes, three large wooden boxes and several black plastic ashtrays. A pack of Marlboro Regulars sits atop each box. An open bottle of Budweiser beer stands on a black stool center stage. A short, dark man enters playing the guitar. Another man—tall, blond, thin—enters, lights a cigarette and begins to speak over the music.)

Folks, I'd like to sing a song about the American dream. About me. About you. About the way our American hearts beat way down in the bottom of our chests. About the special feeling we get in the cockles of our hearts—maybe below the cockles—maybe in the sub-cockle area. Maybe in the liver. Maybe in the kidneys. Maybe even in the colon.

(Singing)

I'm just a regular Joe with a regular job
I'm your average white suburbanite slob
I like football and porno and books about war
I've got an average house with a nice hardwood floor
My wife and my job
My kids and my car
My feet on my table
And a Cuban cigar

But sometimes that just ain't enough
To keep a man like me interested
(Oh no) Uh-uh (no way)
No, I've gotta go out and have fun

1

At someone else's expense
(Oh yeah)
Yeah yeah
(Yeah yeah)
Yeah yeah yeah yeah yeah
I drive really slow in the ultrafast lane,
While people behind me are going insane

I'm an asshole
(He's an asshole)
I'm an asshole
(He's an asshole, such an asshole)

I use public toilets
and I piss on the seat
I walk around in the summertime
Sayin', "How 'bout this heat?"

I'm an asshole
(He's an asshole)
I'm an asshole
(He's the world's biggest asshole)

Sometimes I park in handicapped spaces,
While handicapped people
Make handicapped faces

I'm an asshole
(He's an asshole)
I'm an asshole
(He's a real fucking asshole)

Maybe I shouldn't be singing this song;
Ranting and raving and carrying on.

Maybe they're right when they tell me I'm wrong . . .

Nah

I'm an asshole
(He's an asshole)
I'm an asshole
(He's the world's biggest asshole)

(Screaming, now, the ultimate ugly American) You know what I'm gonna do? I'm gonna get myself a 1967 Cadillac Eldorado convertible—hot pink with whaleskin hubcaps and all-leather cow interior and big brown baby seal eyes for the headlights. I'm gonna drive around in that baby at 115 mph, getting one mile per gallon, sucking down Quarter Pounder cheeseburgers from McDonald's in the old-fashioned nonbiodegradable Styrofoam containers. When I'm done suckin' down those greaseball burgers, I'm gonna toss the Styrofoam container right out the side and there ain't a goddamned thing anybody can do about it. You know why? Because we got the bombs, that's why. Two words: nuclear weapons, okay? Russia, Czechoslovakia, Romania—they can have all the democracy they want. They can have a big democracy cakewalk right through the middle of Tiananmen Square and it won't make a lick of difference because we've got the bombs, okay?

John Wayne's not dead—he's frozen. And as soon as we find the cure for cancer we're gonna thaw out the Duke and he's gonna be pretty pissed off. You know why? Have you ever taken a cold shower? Well, multiply that by 15,000,000 times—that's how pissed off the Duke's gonna be. I'm gonna get the Duke and John Cas-

savetes and Lee Marvin and Sam Peckinpah and a case
of whisky and drive down to Texas . . .

(Hey)
and have a humongous barbecue—
(Hey)
we're gonna go to LBJ's ranch and start a bonfire—
(Hey)
and throw deer and rabbits and cats and old people
and—
(Hey!)
slow drivers and Mickey Rourke and—
(Hey!)
What?
(You know something? You really are an asshole)
Shut up and sing the song.

(He's an asshole)
You empty little simp. I thought I was the ass-
hole—
(He's a real fucking asshole)
And it was him the whole time
(He's an asshole)
I'm an asshole
(He's the world's biggest asshole)
A-S-S-H-O-L-E
(Everybody!)
A-S-S-H-O-L-E
(Barking)
Arf arf arf arf arf arf arf
(Snapping)
Ching fump ching puh fluh cluh bing
Ooh ooh ooh ooh
I'm an asshole and I'm proud of it.

(The tall thin blond man walks off the stage as the lights fade to black)

(Suddenly we hear an offstage announcement)

LADIES AND GENTLEMEN, DUE TO ILLNESS, TONIGHT THE PART OF DENIS LEARY WILL BE PLAYED BY DENIS LEARY. PLEASE WELCOME DENIS LEARY!

(The tall thin blond man enters and lights a cigarette. He takes a deep drag. He enjoys the taste for a moment. He exhales. He picks up the pack and approaches the audience.)

There's a guy, he's English (I don't think we should hold that against him), but apparently he has this life's dream—and I say apparently because he's flying over here with his own money in a couple of weeks to have a Senate hearing and this is what he wants to do: he wants to make the warnings on cigarette packs bigger. He wants the whole front of the pack to be the warning. Like the problem is we haven't noticed yet, right? Like he's gonna get his way and smokers around the world are gonna be going, "Yeah, Bill, I've got some cigarettes— *(Noticing warning on pack)* Hey! Wait a minute. Jesus Christ. These things are bad for you! Shit, I thought they were good for you. I thought they had vitamin C in 'em and stuff." *(Slams pack loudly onto stool)*

You dolt! Doesn't matter how big the warnings are. You could have cigarettes that were called "WARNINGS"; you could have cigarettes that come in a black pack with a skull and crossbones on the front called "TUMORS" and smokers would be lined up around the block saying, "I can't wait to get my hands on these things, can you? I bet you get a tumor as soon as you light up." It doesn't matter how big the warnings are or how much they cost. Keep raising the prices. We'll break into your houses to buy the cigarettes, okay? We're addicted. It's a drug.

You'll have to excuse me. I'm a little hyped up for the show tonight—a little psyched up. I smoked a nice big fat bag of crack right before the show got started! *(Screaming into front row)* ARRGGGHHH!

I'm only kidding, folks. I would never do crack. I would never do a drug named after a part of my own ass.

9

Kind of a personal guideline in my life. Somebody says, "You want some crack?" I say, "I was born with one, pal. I really don't need another one. Thank you very much. If I want the second crack I'll give you a call. But for right now, I'm sticking with the solo crackola. Thank you. If I want to fart in stereo, I'll give you a buzz. For right now, the one crack is fine for the big Irish guy. Thank you."

Crack. Only in New York would a guy invent crack. Only in New York would there be a guy that cocaine wasn't good enough for. One guy walking around the city going, "You know that cocaine is pretty good, but I want something that makes my heart explode as soon as I smoke it, okay? I wanna take one suck off that crack pipe and go *(indicating a chest explosion)*, 'Now I'm happy. I'm dead—the ultimate high.' "

That's the problem with this country. People are never happy with stuff the way it is. They want it bigger, better and stronger and faster. It's the same way with pot. For years pot was just joints. Then bongs came out and bongs were okay too. But then bongs weren't good enough for some people. Remember that friend in high school who wanted to make bongs out of everything? Making bongs out of apples and oranges and stuff? Come in one day and find him going, "Hey look, man, I made a bong out of my *head*. Put the pipe in this ear and suck it out of *this* ear. Go ahead, take a hit." *(He inhales long and loud from his friend's head)* Then they graduate to those big giant bongs you gotta start up like a motorcycle. The kids are driving their bongs down FDR Drive, "Pull the bong over, man. I wanna do a hit." What was the problem with just smoking a joint and eating a couple of Twinkies? Was that a problem?

They say marijuana leads to other drugs. No, it leads to *carpentry*. That's the problem. *(Grabbing box)* Hey. This box could be a bong. This ashtray could be a bong.

(Stepping into the audience and clutching a man's head) This guy's head could be an excellent bong. *(Returning to stage)* Relax. That's why I stopped doing drugs in the first place. Number one, they're bad for you. Number two, I didn't want to build anything. That's why I stopped doing illegal drugs.

Now I just do the legal drugs. Tonight, I'm on NyQuil and Sudafed. Let me tell you something, folks. Forget about cocaine and heroin. All you need is NyQuil and Sudafed. I'm telling you right now, I took the NyQuil five years ago and I just came out of the coma tonight before the show. Claus Von Bulow was standing over my bed going, "Denis, get up! There's something the matter with Sonny! Hurry up!" We've reached the point where over-the-counter drugs are actually stronger than anything you can buy on the streets. It says on the back of the NyQuil box, "May cause drowsiness." It should say, "Don't make any plans, okay? Kiss your family and friends good-bye and say hello to Claus!" I love NyQuil. It's the best drug ever invented. Capital N, small y, big Q il. *(Chanting)* NyQuil, NyQuil, NyQuil—we love you! Sing the NyQuil song with me. Sing! NyQuil's like an old friend, like a comfy chair. It's never changed. Not like the other cold medicines. They're all changing now: "We know there's a small child inside of you who wants to taste grape, cherry and orange flavor." Not NyQuil! They still have the original green-death flavor. You know why? Because it's so strong, you take one shot and you go, "This tastes like . . ." BANG! You're in a coma already! NyQuil is also a good loophole option for all you people in those twelve-step recovery programs. "NyQuil —the thirteenth step in your twelve-step recovery program." Suck down as much as you want! "You're drunk!"

"I am not. I have a cold!"

Soon the streets will be clogged with people in ragged

clothes sticking out their green tongues, "Got any change, man? I got the flu. C'mon. I got it bad, man. Sinuses are all congested. Please help."

The cold medicine revolution. People at parties opening up capsules of Contac and snorting the contents through rolled-up dollar bills. "Sure I'm fucked up but I haven't coughed or sneezed in fifteen years."

I think we need something stronger than NyQuil. We need a medicine that guarantees a coma. We need "New COMA!" You might never wake up! Wouldn't that be nice? You know when your life sucks? When your job is getting to you, the bills are piling up, the muscles in your neck are glommed into a tight-fisted ball—you suck down a shot of COMA and get three, four, five years of sleep. Wouldn't that be nice? Because when you come out of the coma, your family loves you. Oh yeah, they're happy to have you back. You can get away with anything then. Burn the house down, eat the dog—they are happy as hell.

"Ma. I'm sorry I slept with Grandma."

"Don't worry, son. At least you're not in that coma."

Remember Karen Anne Quinlan? She was in a coma for nine years. Nine years. A decade minus one. She missed every episode of "Cheers." Finally, her parents couldn't take it anymore. They went to court and got permission and they pulled the plug. They pulled the plug! And four days later—she woke up.

That must've been a nice surprise. The parents are in the room. They've got the parish priest with them. He's in the corner filching through the sports page and muttering, "God has a plan blah blah blah . . . We all have to go blah blah blah" on the death watch, pricing coffins, flowers, et cetera and then—"Hi, Dad!" *(Dad is very surprised)* "Hi, honey! Did I unplug you? I meant to unplug the TV! *(To Mom)* Get the doctor—she's up, for crissakes. *(To Karen)* Didja sleep well, honey? Here. Have some candy. *(Urgently)* Get the doctor! I can't believe we gave her kidneys away. Get the doctor! *(To Karen)* You wanna watch TV? We got cable put in."

Comas are expensive. You've got to plug in cords. You've got to pay the electric bill. You've got to have round-the-clock nurses. That's why the aneurism is the way to go. Your head blows up and the whole thing is over with.

Don't you wish you could have a brain hemorrhage whenever you wanted to? That would be an extra added bonus. A built-in human body ejection seat. An out door. All you have to do is think really hard, close your eyes and BLAM! You are gone.

You're at the office, behind your desk, bored, bent, broken. It's a beautiful day outside. You want to go hiking. You close your eyes. You concentrate and BLAM! Your head blows up. They have to send you home. You can't sit around answering phones all day—you have no head. You'd just be holding the phone up where your head used to be—waving it above your neck—people on the other end of the line going, "Hello? Hello? Must be one of those headless people. They shouldn't even have jobs."

Help the headless. See? You'll even get sympathy. All the antiheadless people—all the people with heads—will abuse and ignore you and then—the government will step in to answer the pleas of the headless and their supporters and soon there will be prosthetic heads you can screw on and headless hotlines and special dogs with huge furry heads who walk beside you and see *everything*. You'll get the government grants and free food and special vans with sensor headlights that act as eyeballs—you'll drive and eat and visit Alaska!

They never told us about aneurisms growing up, did

they? They told you a stick could poke out your eye, they told you strangers might offer you candy, they told you not to go swimming for at least one hour after eating a sandwich. But they never, ever once mentioned that your head could suddenly, unexpectedly, unannounced— explode. You had to discover it the weasel way. You're fourteen. You've got acne. Your parents are getting dressed up to go to a wake. "Mr. Carelli died." How? They pause. They look at each other. Heart attack? Car accident? They pause again. They look at you. They judge you old enough. "A blood vessel burst in his head." What? What the fuck? I've got acne, a constant erection, no money of my own and now you tell me my head could blow up? At any given moment? Great. Thanks. For two years I was afraid to do anything. Afraid to get my heart beating too fast in case some synapse in my brain would snap and clog a vessel. I walked very slowly. No running. No smoking. No jerking off. To this day, I'm still very careful when I have sex. "Did you come?" No. But at least my head didn't blow up.

Help the headless, folks. Sure they can drink. But they can't read. Help the headless. Help the homeless. Help the headless homeless. Almost everyone who's headless is homeless. Because once the head blows up, they can't remember where they live.

(Lights up cigarette and inhales deeply. Pauses. Exhales loudly.)

Drugs. I did my share. I did more than my share. I did *my* share *(pointing into the audience)* plus yours and yours and yours and—I did enough for the first three rows. Drugs, boy—capital D.

I grew up in the seventies. That's when drugs were drugs. We did it all. Cocaine and marijuana—that was child's play to us. We did stuff that people don't even do anymore! Remember ludes? Like ludes. Quaaludes. Ludes, man. Fucking luuuudes!

I think ludes explain why we were wearing the giant-flare-bell-bottom pants and the platform shoes. What do you think? I think it's the only *possible* explanation. There we were in the middle of a sexual revolution wearing clothing that guaranteed we wouldn't get laid. *(Gazing down at feet)* "Wow. This is it. I'm definitely getting laid tonight. I can't see my ankles. I can't see my shoes. That's what women want—men without feet."

See, that was the thing in the mid-seventies. The bell-bottoms took over and the only way you could be a cooler guy was to get bigger bell-bottoms. We used to sit around and get high and go, "Man, when I get some money I'm getting the biggest bell-bottoms in history, man. They're going to start at my neck and go twenty feet straight out. I'm going to be surrounded by ninety feet of fuckin' bell-bottoms. Homeless people are gonna be living under my pants, man! I'll have platform shoes and be twenty feet tall."

Sex in the seventies was not even sex. It went beyond coupling and mating. It moved into the area of aerobics. Simple exercise. No commitment. No conversation. No disease. The worst worry we had was herpes. God, remember herpes? Back then a red sore on your lip was like having a scarlet capital A sewn onto your chest. People would cross the street muttering to each other, "Herpes. Tragic, really." Now if all you have is herpes you are a hero. "Just herpes? That's all? I think I'm in love. Let's fuck."

Most of the time the biggest piece of luggage sex carried with it back in the seventies was the clap—gonorrhea, syphilis. Those were the big ones. You used to get really pissed if you caught a case. "Christ! You gave me the clap. Now I gotta go all the way down to the clinic, get a shot in my ass. It's probably gonna cost me twenty-five bucks!" Now it could cost you your life. Hey—lemme tell you something—I love sex. It's great. But I never remember seeing a woman across a crowded room and thinking, "Now she's worth dying for." Maybe after twenty years together—love, bonding, et cetera—but certainly not as a one-night stand. Hey, I even wash my hands after I jerk off. I don't trust anyone.

Masturbation is the comeback player of the decade, man. It's quick, it's fun and you live longer. All those dorks who couldn't get laid in high school? Those are the cool guys now. Those are the guys at the wakes going, "It's a shame, isn't it? Hey—have you seen the new issue of *Shaved Beaver?*" Back in the seventies we didn't have time to masturbate. We were too busy engaging in the actual act. You could start having sex with someone before you knew their name. Names? Hah! You can find out stuff like that later. Find out while you're doing it. *(In the midst of intercourse)* "So, you from around here? A little lower. That's good. Yeah. What's yer name again? Susan. Right."

And if you were really worried about the clap, have the doctor right in the room with you. Throw him some extra cabbage. Have him stick that needle into your ass as soon as you come. *(Coming)* "Oh! Ohhhhh . . . ah . . . Hit me, Doc. . . . Ow. Great. Let's get something to eat."

The seventies. Sex with anything that moved. And some things that didn't. Sex and drugs and more sex and more drugs and shots in the ass and more drugs and shots in the ass and more drugs and a little more sex and then just a bit of rock 'n' roll before we pass out and wake up to find Reagan is President. "What? Hey, you guys, get up! Get up! Reagan is President! Call the

Betty Ford Center. We shoulda known, man. They let us do all the drugs and have unlimited sex so we would forget to vote. They caught us with our pants down."

We did it all in the seventies. We even invented a couple of drugs. That's how desperate we were to get high. Remember "whippets"? *(Judging audience reaction)* See? Some people laugh and the others need an explanation. Whippets came about in the seventies when some kid took the time, used his imagination and figured out an entirely new way to get high. This kid should have been involved in the space program. One day this kid went down to the supermarket, picked up an aerosol can of whipped cream and discovered that, when you press the nozzle on the top, some gas escapes before the whipped cream comes out. You snort the gas and you get high for five seconds. We didn't have MTV—we had the supermarket! We were down there every day and if they were out of whipped cream we snorted hamburger. We didn't care. We *had* to get high. We had to get over that bell-bottom hump.

Boy, we did so many drugs in the seventies. We didn't realize the damage we were doing. We just didn't know —because we were so fucked up. Kids like me made the Grateful Dead the richest band in history. We would eat acid and eat mushrooms and smoke pot and snort coke and drink and go to their shows. I don't even think they brought their instruments. "Just pretend you're playing, man. They don't know the difference." *(Staring off into the distance. Dazed.)* "Wow, man. Jerry is playing an invisible guitar, man! Look at the size of his bell-bottoms. Wow!" That's how you gauged how good a concert was back in the seventies: how fucked up you were, right?

"How was the Aerosmith gig?"

"It was fuckin' unbelievable, man. I sucked down a bottle of schnapps and drank a case of beer and puked and passed out. I missed the whole thing. It was excellent, man. I've gotta buy the live album.

"I went to see Zeppelin, right? Me and Head and Fitzy and Sully and Gronk, right? So we stop and get some beers and Fitzy says he's got some acid so we eat it, right? And then Sully says he's got some blow so we snort it. It was speedy. Matter of fact, it was *really* fuckin' speedy. So Gronk says he's got some speed. So we do that. It wasn't speedy at all. Just made our gums numb. My mouth—my whole mouth—my gums, my teeth, my lips, my tongue—I can't feel any of 'em. So Head says to Gronk, 'Hey, this ain't speed. This is coke. You got ripped off.' So Gronk says, 'Thagathathum.' His whole mouth's frozen from the speed that was probably coke and he's all hopped up from the coke that was probably speed so he's a mess like the rest of us so Head says he has some wicked good pot so we do a bunch of bong hits—Head has this excellent bong made outta this kidney stone his old man passed last year—thing comes right out through his dad's dick—intense, man—I mean, you're doing a bong hit and you're looking at it and you're thinking, 'Man, this had to hurt.' So anyway, to make a long story short, we cross the median and crash head on into an eighteen wheeler. Sully's dead, Gronk is paralyzed from the nose down, Head's arms are cut off and Fitzy was thrown from the car—we never found him. It was excellent, man. We're gonna go see 'em next month. Fuckin' Jimmy Page. Robert Plant. Awesome."

(Higher) "I saw Dylan, man. Well, I didn't really see him. I ate some 'shrooms and some ludes and smoked some hash right before I went to the gig. So I saw like, big pink lizards and blue angels and Abraham Lincoln and Rudolf Hess and Yogi Berra but they sounded like Dylan so I musta been at the right place. Even if it

wasn't, it was an excellent show, man. Lincoln was unbelievable."

I remember coming home from a softball game and
chomping down five brownies that were in this pan on
the stove because I was in a rush to get to this Roxy
Music gig and I jumped into the shower and got dressed
and my roommate, a guy named Robert Will whose nick-
name was Space—which should've been a sign—a big
neon sign—says, " 'Djoo eat them brownies?" and I say
yeah and he says, "Shit, man, there's about two pounds
of excellent hash in them brownies," and I go, "great," so
anyway, to make a long story short—I'm sitting next to
Lee Harvey Oswald at the gig and Roxy Music is onstage but all I can hear is the sound of my own heartbeat
—really loud—no music—nothing—just THA-THUMP
THA-THUMP THA-THUMP THA-THUMP over and
over, so Oswald turns to me and says, "You wanna keep
it down?" I always thought he was an asshole. So I don't
give a shit. I let my heart beat as loud as it wants THA-
THUMP THA-THUMP and Oswald's getting really
pissed and I don't care because whether he shot him or
not he's partially responsible for JFK's death and besides
I always thought he'd be more of a heavy metal fan and
he's here at this Roxy Music gig and then suddenly I
notice Space coming down the aisle toward us with Jack
Ruby and four beers and I snap, "I can't take it anymore," so I rush out into the lobby and I grab a cop and I
say, "You gotta help me. I'm having a heart attack," and
he says "You're not having a heart attack." And I say,
"Oh yeah? Listen." And I hold up my shirt and you can
hear it loud and clear THA-THUMP THA-THUMP and
he just walks away so I jump in a cab and rush back to
the apartment and get in bed and I'm afraid to go to
sleep in case my heart explodes so I turn on the TV and

the only thing on is *Oklahoma!*—that horrible musical—
so for hours I lie sweating and squirming and listening to
my heart go THA-THUMP THA-THUMP and *(singing)*
"Ooooooooook—lahoma where the wind comes whipping
through the trees!" THA-THUMP THA-THUMP.

We did all the drugs. We did 'em all. Cocaine, we
started that, that was us back in the late seventies.
You're welcome. What a great drug cocaine was. What a
great high. "I'd like to do some coke. I'd like to do a drug
that makes my penis small, makes my heart explode,
makes my nose bleed and sucks all my money out of the
bank. Is that possible, please? I'd like to sweat for seven
hours in a bathroom. Is that possible? I'd like to talk to
complete idiots about nothing for fifteen hours straight.
With no penis and a nosebleed, can I do that, please?
Where do I sign up?" That should have been the warning
sign with coke: when you were in the bathroom with
some complete asshole jabbering away because he had
the coke. If Hitler had coke there would be Jews in the
bathroom going *(SNORT)*, "I know you didn't do it.
(SNORT) Fucking Mussolini. *(SNORT)* I *like* your mus-
tache. *(SNORT)*."

Cocaine. The big lie. Tell me about it. "This stuff's directly from Colombia. Hasn't been stepped on at all."
Yeah, right. And Liberace died of emphysema. Yeah,
yeah. The best pitch I ever heard about cocaine was back
in the early eighties a street dealer on the Lower East
Side followed me down the sidewalk going, "I got some
great blow, man. I got the shit that killed Belushi." This
was two days after Belushi kicked. Man. Talk about mar-
keting. You got any blow? "Yeah. Whaddaya want? Belushi? Bias? Keith Moon?"

Remember when we thought cocaine was harmless?
Just a recreational drug, that's all. You would actually
have the discussion with your friends while you were

doing the blow. *(SNORT)* "This stuff's addictive." *(SNORT)* "No, it's not." *(SNORT)* "Yes, it is." *(SNORT)* "No, it's not. I've been doing it every night for fifteen years—it's not addictive!" *(SNORT)*

Eight-balls. Remember eight-balls? This was three and a half grams of coke packaged as one and sold at a discount. It was mostly groups of men who did eight-balls. Five guys sitting around on a Friday night. Around eight o'clock. One guy says, "Hey! Let's get an eight-ball. It'll last us all weekend!" Yeah. Eleven o'clock you have five guys who are speeding their brains out going, "Letsgetanothereightballc'mon."

Groups of people would go to parties with cocaine, sharing it among themselves—maybe four people—sneaking into the bathroom or a spare bedroom—snorting the blow—and then walking around and trying to act as if they're not high. Walking around the party with that Mr. Ed mouth with the lips snapped back taut, teeth grinding, the ring of white around the nostrils. "Are you doing blow?" "No. No. Just drank a pot of coffee. Had my wisdom teeth out. Broke my jaw, it's wired together. Gotta go to the bathroom again. I'm on this special medication. For the wisdom teeth jaw thing."

That's the lure of drugs, though. That's the temptation. The long wicked whisper that sucks you in. "Get fucked up. Forget about your problems. Escape." And you can. For hours at a time. Escape completely. Snort a gram. Shoot a load. Suck down a liter bottle. Dance. Fuck. Listen to an entire Led Zeppelin boxed set. Through headphones. With the Super Bass pumped all the way up. But no matter how fucked up you get . . . no matter how far you run . . . no matter how long the crash—when you wake up, your problems are still there. Staring you right in the face. *(Smiling)* "Hi. Good morning. Boy, you were out like a light. Oh. I'm sorry. How rude of me. I'm reality. *(Indicating others)* This is Love, this is Sex, this is The Past, this is The Future and that big guy in the back—that's Death. He was really pissed at you. He almost took you last night. But he didn't. So here we are. Umm . . . tell you what. You go back to sleep and we'll be out in the kitchen making coffee. Sleep as long as you want. We'll be right here waiting for you, okay? Oh, by the way. You know that they're turning the phone off at five today? Oh, and there's a spot on your left lung and—oh, never mind. Go back to sleep and we'll hash it all out later. Hash. Hah. Get it?"

Yeah. For a while there we thought we were gonna outrun 'em all, didn't we? Coke was getting cheaper. So was heroin. Money was appearing out of nowhere. You could do tons of drugs and still buy stuff for the house.

Then in the mid-eighties society caught up with us. They came up with that little campaign, "Say No to Drugs." Remember what a success that was? If they wanted to do an advertising campaign about drugs, they should have based it on our experience. We did drugs for a couple of years back in the seventies and look at the clothes we ended up wearing. There's your advertising campaign right there. *(Indicating straight-leg jeans)* "These are your pants. *(Indicating bell-bottoms)* These are your pants on drugs. Now don't do them. Do you want to listen to K.C. & the Sunshine Band? No, you don't. You wanna wear a big satin shirt with a unicorn on the front and giant flying-nun collar? No, you don't. Now come on! Two words: Jethro Tull. Okay? Two more words: Aqua Lung. Now put down those drugs." People go, "Oh, geez, you know, why didn't you go into rehab or something?" We didn't have rehab in the seventies. Everybody was doing drugs. We were doing 'em. Our parents were doing 'em. Rock stars were doing 'em. Everybody. We never even heard of rehab in the seventies.

Back in the seventies rehab meant you just stopped smoking pot for a couple of days, you know? "Give me a case of Budweiser. I've gotta slow down. I'm out of control. Look at the size of my pants, for Christ's sake! Who the hell do I think I am?"

Now the big celebrity thing is rehab. All you've got to do is wake up hating your parents one day, abuse alcohol and drugs for a while, go into rehab and come out and you're on the cover of *People* magazine. You're talking to Larry King and Sally Raphael. I thought show business was toil plus talent—you take some acting classes, you study faces, accents, gestures—you work your way slowly up that show-business ladder. I didn't know you had to come from a fucked-up family.

I come from a normal family. I'm afraid I'm not gonna make it now. I'm gonna sue my parents. "Why didn't you screw me up more when I was a kid, for crissakes? Why didn't you let Uncle Connie feel me up at that wedding when I was five years old? I can't even get a part in a sitcom now. Remember Jimmy O'Connell? From down the street? His mother slept with him when we were in high school and now he's a regular on 'Murphy Brown.'" Everybody comes from a dysfunctional family now.

(Lights up cigarette. Inhales. Exhales.) Celebrity rehab. Democracy in action. People need help. Celebrities need private help. Designer drunk tanks. The Betty Ford Center—where compassion and support and healing depend on whether or not your development deal with Tri-Star has been canceled.

(On phone)

"Betty Ford Center. Can I help you?"
"Yeah. I need help. Please."
"Who is this?"

"I need help bad. I'm strung out."

"God. Your voice sounds so familiar. Is this Sally Fields?"

(Crying now) "I've been coked up for two weeks straight, I—"

"Sean Young! I knew it! I *knew* you had to be on drugs."

"This is Drew Barrymore! Sean Young? Gimme a little credit."

"Drew Barrymore? God. You were great in *E.T.* So cute."

"Thank you."

"And I loved that scene where E.T. hides in the closet with all the stuffed toys and then you walk in."

"That was my idea."

"Really? And I read about you in *People* magazine. Getting drunk and doing drugs when you were ten years old? God."

"Well, look. I just had another slip. I'm really fucked up. I'm at the Mayflower Hotel in New York and I thought I would just fly out and check in."

"Oh. Well, gee, Drew, I uhh—"

"What?"

"Well . . . it's been a long time since *E.T.*"

"Excuse me?"

"Don't get me wrong. It was a wonderful piece of work, especially for such a young actress. But it was over ten years ago."

"I don't *believe* this."

"Do you have anything coming up?"

"No."

"Oh. That's too bad. I'm sure you understand. We like to keep up a certain level here. We can't let just anybody in. Next thing you know, we'd have sitcom stars and character actors and the soaps banging on the door."

"This is ridiculous."

"I mean, we don't mind a Mary Tyler Moore or Liz Taylor—someone who may not be working but carries a high profile. But we have to draw the line somewhere. We got a call from that guy from 'Cheers'—the one with the coke problem—last week he says he had a slip. Well, hey, pal. Call your mother, y'know? It's not our fault you settled for TV."

"Well, just what do you suggest I do?"

"I'd say call Spielberg and see if he can get you a part in his new project. Then go on a big coke bender, call us, we'll book you for thirty days, then we can tie the publicity about your sobriety right into the film's release. Probably get the cover of *People* with that one. 'She's Back and She's Better!' Nice photo of you in a leather bike jacket, blond highlights."

"All right. But let me talk to my agent first."

"Okay. Have you seen *Silence of the Lambs* yet?"

"No."

"Excellent. Jodie Foster. God, I'd love to get her in here. We'd be all over the paper. Bye."

Everybody comes from a dysfunctional family now. Everyone. Roseanne Barr comes from a dysfunctional family? Not *Roseanne*—she seems so normal to me. And the Jacksons were dysfunctional? Not the *Jacksons!* Come on. These people give each other new *heads* for Christmas!

"Here, Michael. Here's your new head."

"Oh, thank you. It's whiter than the last one. I'll look just like a white guy!"

Is there any such thing as a functional family? Does it exist? "The Brady Bunch." Was that functional? I don't think so. I never trusted Alice. I think she wanted to sleep with everyone in the house.

Even Jesus came from a dysfunctional family. Father

and mother aren't having sex. Mother gets pregnant outside the marriage. No wonder he was wandering the countryside with a bottomless jug of wine. *(Staggering)* "You dunno me! I'm the Messiah!"

The newest theory on the self-help front is the Inner Child. I'm sure you've heard of it. This theory holds that you probably came from a dysfunctional family and your childhood was a mess because your parents didn't give you enough love and attention.

Wow.

So this is where we get off the Sigmund Freud Turnpike? At The Child Inside Me exit? Let's say for the sake of argument that there is a small child inside of all of us —my wife is seven months pregnant so I assume she's eating for three now. Does the child get into movies free? Do we have to buy presents for the inner child at Christmastime? I'm pretty sure I can take my inner child in a fistfight.

Some people have found the child inside themselves and moved on to find the man inside and the fire in the belly and—hey, it's getting mighty crowded in there. This probably explains those lower back pains I've been having.

There are now groups of grown men going on self-discovery weekends, marching into the mountains, joining hands in moonlit forests, howling and beating drums. They pay money to do this. Personally, I like to do the same thing in my living room while I'm watching the Super Bowl. But I do it alone.

Two words, folks: circle jerk. Two more words: not me.

I knew that once we got on this self-help escalator we wouldn't be able to get off. It's the seventies coming back to haunt us. Once we crash-landed and saw Reagan we panicked. We rifled through our drawers looking for evidence and explanations and we came across the photos of ourselves in the platform shoes and the bell-bottoms and the shirts and we called for help.

(Fevered) "Doc. You gotta help me. There's something wrong. Look at these clothes."

Soon everybody was quitting drugs and drink and joining support groups—Alcoholics Anonymous, Narcotics Anonymous, Coughaholics Anonymous. "My name is Bill, and I can't stop drinking Formula 44D."

Soon we had flocks of books extolling every kind of dysfunctional behavior and its corresponding correction.

Men Who Hate Women and the Women Who Love Them, Women Who Hate Men Who Hate Trucks, Dogs Who Hate Cats, Men Who Hate Hats, Hats and the Women Who Love Them, Women Who Hate Men Who Hate Hats.

I hate them all.

I hate the women who hate the men who hate the hats.

I hate the mewling and the maw.

I hate the obsession with confession this whole country has.

(In announcer's voice)

MEN WHO DRESS UP LIKE CHICKENS AND FUCK THEIR OWN KIDS—TODAY ON "OPRAH" . . . KIDS WHO DRESS UP LIKE MEN AND FUCK CHICKENS . . . KIDS WHO FUCK MEN WHO FUCK CHICKENS—TODAY ON "OPRAH."

I hate Oprah. I hate Phil. I hate Marlo Thomas. I hate Danny Thomas. I hate the Thomas family. I hate St. Jude.

Yeah, I know, I know. I'm in denial. I keep denying the cold hard fact that I could buy an automatic rifle for twenty-five bucks and take a couple of hostages. That's how they'll find me. Naked on a rooftop with a bag of crack and an Uzi and Sally Jessy Raphael in a headlock.

I will not bond. I will not share. I refuse to nurture.

Now everyone seems to be pointing the finger at the easiest target: Mom and Dad. *(Whining)* "I became an alcoholic because my parents didn't love me enough. They used to hit me and stuff." Hey, my parents used to beat the shit out of me. And, looking back on it, I'm glad they did. And I'm looking forward to beating the shit out of my own kids. For no reason whatsoever.

BAM!

"Ow! Whaddya hittin' me for?"

"Because you're my kid. Now get out there and mow the lawn!"

There's therapy for you. Mowing the lawn and crying at the same time. *(Circles the stage mowing and crying)*

(Peering out window) "The Leary kid's in therapy again. Their lawn looks great! Maybe we should send our kids over to their house."

These people with their personal baggage, their Gucci Therapy Luggage that they drag all over everyone else's feet. *(More whining)* "My life didn't turn out the way I thought it would." Hey. Join the club. I thought I was gonna be starting center fielder for the Boston Red Sox. Life sucks. Get a helmet.

Look, you are an alcoholic because you like to drink. You are a junkie because you like to shoot smack. That's it. Case closed. Final score: Drugs 10–Belushi 0.

"But I'm just not happy." Hey! *(SLAP)* HEY! *(SLAP)* HEY HEY HEY! *(BANG SLAP BANG)* No-body* is happy! *I'm* not happy. *(Pointing into audience)* *He's* not happy. She's not happy, she's not happy, *they're* not happy. This guy is miserable. This is probably the best he ever feels.

Fucked up or fucked over, sober or straight, happiness

comes in small doses. The five-second orgasm, the last chocolate chip cookie. You come, you eat it, you sigh, you feel guilty, you fall asleep, you get up in the morning and you go to work. That's it, folks. Case closed. Final score: Cookie 12–You 0.

This country needs to sit down and shut up. It's about time we realized that nobody is happy. Canada's not happy, Russia's not happy, China's not happy. Maybe we've all taken the American dream a little bit too far. It was originally supposed to be simple. Freedom of speech and the pursuit of happiness. And happiness meant you built a little cabin, you got a horse, a piece of land and an outhouse in the backyard. That was it. Sure it sucked. But you had freedom of speech so you could complain about it all you wanted. Now we've gotten unrealistic. Now we've got a new agenda. Freedom of speech doesn't carry any weight anymore.

You can walk down the street in New York City and eat ten different kinds of ethnic food on one block. Wow. Stop and think about that sometime. Maybe some night when you're sitting naked on the couch watching three different movies at once—*The Godfather Part III* on HBO, *Meet John Doe* on Cinemax and *Frankenhooker*—which you rented and which you are fast forwarding and checking in on every once in a while so you can see the nude scenes—and you get hungry and you mull over the choices—Italian, Mexican, Greek diner, Thai, Vietnamese, McDonald's—and you decide on Chinese and you call down and order and fifteen minutes later a small Chinese kid appears at the door and asks for ten dollars. Ten bucks! It would only have been seven but you had him bring up a two-liter bottle of Coke too. Ten bucks.

For twelve bucks they'd probably throw in a blow job. C'mon. This stuff was not written into the Constitution, folks. These are bonuses. In Ethiopia, when a father turns to his son and says, "Whaddaya want to do when you grow up?" nine out of ten times the kid says, "Eat."

Everybody wants the same things in America. Everybody wants the house and the car and the picket fence. Well, there's more to life than that. A lot more. There's the pool and the boat and the summer house. There's Armani suits and leather sofas.

You know what I want? I want it all. I want the house, the car, the wife, the kids. I want the picket fence and the pool—the big kidney-shaped pool. I want a CD player. I want a Sony E.S. CDP 77 Multichanger System with wireless remote so I can dump seven CDs in it— Sinatra, Nirvana, Latifah—and listen all day. I want a Mitsubishi C.S. 76-inch Improved Definition Picture-In-Picture wall-mounted TV with the little box up in the corner of the screen so I can watch two shows at once.

I want a missile launcher. I want a Patriot missile launcher—I pay my taxes—why can't I have one? I want to launch missiles from my backyard. I want to sit in a fluorescent yellow raft in my official NFL Orange Starter swimming trunks in my kidney-shaped pool and attack Canada. I want to videotape it on my hand-held Sony Handicam and play it back on my Mitsubishi 76-inch while I'm watching the Super Bowl in the little box in the corner of the screen and listening to the Led Zeppelin Digitally Remastered CD Box Set.

I want Michael Jackson's nose. I want Michael Jackson's original nose mounted on a plaque and hung in my living room.

I want new sneakers. Not Air Jordans. Air Birds. I don't wanna jump high and run fast. I want Air Birds. I want shoes that actually have a gravity pull so I can only jump six inches off the ground—sneakers that suck you back down to earth if you try to jump seven inches.

I want a helmet. A cheese helmet. A helmet full of cheese. You just pop it on your head and eat all day.

I want it all, folks. I want it all and I want it now and I'm gonna get it with or without your help. I think you know what I'm talking about. I think you hear me knocking and I think I'm coming in and you know what? I'm already wearing the cheese helmet.

(Lights up cigarette and takes several deep drags. Stares at audience for a moment. Takes a few more drags. Paces a bit. Exhales an enormous cloud of smoke.)

Happy people suck. They are annoying. They're just too goddamn happy. *(Smiling and waving)* "Have a nice day!" Have a coronary embolism, you empty little simp. Anyone who is that happy must be an idiot, because if you can read and there's a newspaper stand near your house—you have nothing to be happy about. I don't trust happy people. I think anyone with a big smile on their face during daylight should be timed with a radar gun— and if the smile lasts longer than three seconds, give them a urine test. *(Gazing into glass of urine)* "Ahh . . . just as we thought. You are a complete and utter moron. We're going to have to shoot you." BLAM!

Why aren't the happy people forced into therapy? They're the ones in the minority. They're the ones screwing it up for the rest of us. Let's put them into support groups. *(Smiling)* "My name is Bob, and I can't stop smiling. I love life. I can't wait to get up in the morning and greet the new day. I have a tight, firm regular bowel movement every day at 10 A.M. I haven't used toilet paper since I was seven. Please help me."

Maybe this happiness and inner child and self-analysis and disappointment and high expectation business is all a matter of how you look at it. Roseanne Barr has a dream where she sees her father coming at her with lust on his lips and malice in his eyes. I see my father coming at me with a shovel saying, "It snowed last night. Dig out the car."

DRINK

(Grabs beer off stool and raises it up in toast) Here's to Kitty Dukakis. *(Chugs half of the beer and places it back on stool)* You know what I'm talking about, folks. C'mon! You know the story. Kitty Dukakis lost her access to alcohol in public because her husband became a public figure. So did you read her book? Inspirational! Did you read the list of stuff she was drinking in place of store-bought alcohol? Mouthwash—mmmmm. Nail polish— *(licking lips)* mmmmmm-mmm. Cutting open roll-on antiperspirant bottles and drinking the fluid out of the bottom—*(rubbing stomach)* Yeah! Here's a woman who knows how to party.

"Kitty—we're out of booze!"

"So what? Open up the medicine cabinet!"

I think society has the same problem with alcohol it has with drugs. If they had left alcohol alone I think it would have been fine. Alcohol was fine when it was the four basic groups: beer, gin, whiskey and vodka. Then you had to like the taste of it. You've all made that whiskey face. You can't take a shot of good whiskey without making that face. You've seen those old men sitting around in bars making that permanent whiskey face. *(Takes shot of whiskey and forms wide frozen grimace)* "How ya doin? Jesus. Fuckin' Giants, huh?" So how did you get around that problem? Schnapps, the crack of alcohol. "For all the people who don't like the taste of alcohol but love the taste of candy: Schnapps!" You've all had that Satan-schnapps experience where you go out with somebody to have a couple of relaxing drinks and they're drinking schnapps. Apparently there's only one way to drink that stuff: bang-shots. One after the other: bang! bang! bang!

"Bill, slow down."

"It's just schnapps. What harm can it do?" Bang, bang, bang, bang!

Two hours later you're driving home with the Tasmanian Devil in the back seat of the car. *(Screaming and flailing about)* "We gotta get him home." He wakes up the next morning and his liver is sitting next to him having a cup of coffee, going, "You're an asshole. You know that?" *(To liver)* "Get back in my body."

I'm Irish. You know our relationship with alcohol. Everybody has their little ethnic table they have to sit at and that's ours. The happy, drunken Irish guys.

The happy, drunken, angry-for-a-second-but-then-happy-again Irish guys.

The happy, drunken, angry - for - a - second - then - really - pissed - off - and - punching - out - his - cousin - and - swearing - at - the - bartender's - girlfriend - then - apologizing - and - buying - drinks - for - everyone - and - crying - and - then - punching - his - cousin - and - punching - the - bartender - and - crying - and - apologizing - and - not - understanding - why - he's - getting - thrown - out - then - cursing - and - screaming - and - threatening - everyone - and - wanting - his - drink - brought - out - to - the - street - then - punching - a - cop - and - getting - arrested - for - the - third - time - this - week—Irish guys.

There are a lot of reasons offered up as to why the Irish drink so much. "It's the sorrow of the state of our beautiful little island—no money. . . . It's the repression—for years we were stepped on by England—kept down, starved to death. . . . It's the pain of the past."

I think it's the music. Have you ever heard a happy Irish song? No. It doesn't exist. From the beginning of time all the way up to U2—there has never been a happy Irish song. It's always the same:

(Sings in a dirgelike rhythm)

"They come over here and they take all our land.
They chop off our heads and they boil them in oil.
Our children are leaving and we have no heads—
We drink and we sing and we drink and we die."

"Geez, guys. Can't you play a happy number?"
"You want a happy number? We'll play it a little faster."

(Singing in a jaunty jiglike rhythm)

"They come over here and they chop off our legs.
They cut off our hands and put nails in our eyes.
O'Grady is dead and O'Hanrahan's gone.
We drink and we die and continue to drink."

"Thanks, guys. That's much better. I'll have a beer, and a vat of whiskey and some teeth and a gun, please?" No wonder everyone's afraid of the IRA. Violent political revolutionaries driving around in black vans with explosive latex, pipe bombs and three cases of Guinness.

(Drunk behind the wheel)

"What was the number of that building?"
"I dunno. Thirteen? Fifteen? Pull over, I gotta piss."
KER-BLAM!
They want us to stop drinking and driving. I always thought that was a good idea—stopping it. But they go about it all the wrong way. What did the government come up with? D.D. Designated Driver. Just like Just Say No to Drugs—only better. We're not saying you can't drink—well, we *are* saying that you can't drink. But your friends can! And you drive them around!

This doesn't work. We've all been in a crowded restaurant or nightclub and seen that table with twelve people seated. Eleven happy, drunken people and one really bummed-out guy? The guy at the end of the table. The sweaty guy with the pot of coffee and the "Not Me. I'm Driving" button pinned to his chest. The guy going, "I hate these people. I gotta drive these shit-faced assholes home. I'm killing everybody even though I'm sober. I'm gonna drive us all right into a tree!"

Designated drivers should be forced to drink. And the stats will back me up. Every time you read about alcohol-related accidents, who's the guy that walks away alive? The drunk guy. The guy who sucks down eighteen quarts of beer, drives into a brick wall at 107 miles per hour and walks away from the accident.

(Slamming door behind himself, staggering) "Damn car sucks, man! I'm walkin' home. Let's go."

They find the sober guy folded up into the glove compartment. "Here he is." *(Holding remains in the palm of his hand)* "Too bad he didn't drink."

I'm glad A.A. became such a big thing because I have a couple of friends who would be dead without it. But now we have a different problem. Now we have people quitting drinking and drugs and in place of that they're working out. Bad decision. See, I'm not a workout guy, folks. I walk and I smoke. That's about it, you know? I'm a softball guy. I love softball. Softball is just baseball with beer. That's why they make the ball so big—so you can see it when you're shitfaced. I understood Nautilus. I didn't do it, but when it first came into style it made sense to me. There were arm machines for the arms and leg machines for the legs. But have you seen these people who are using the Stairmasters? Have we turned into gerbils, ladies and gentlemen? People are paying money to go into a room and walk up three steps over and over again for an hour and a half. You can do this at home for free! Move into a fifth-floor walk-up on the Lower East Side and you can walk up and down stairs all day! What's next, the chairmaster? I sit down. I get up. I sit down. I get up. The doormaster! I open the door. I close the door. What's going on?

So now you have these people who are quitting drinking and drugs. They're completely stressed out, but they're working out in place of that. You've seen those people walking around Manhattan, with the really stressed-out face going a million miles an hour. "I've got a lot of stuff to do. Yeah, I'm unhappy but I'm in great shape. So I'll be unhappy until I'm ninety-six years old!"

You think people are stressed out now. Wait until the first generation of crack babies hit the service industries of America. In about fifteen years we're gonna have waiters and waitresses and cabdrivers and doormen foaming at the mouth and barking at us, "ARF! ARF! ARF! ARF ARF ARF!" *(Scared)* "Sixty-eighth and Broadway, please."

I guess I'm a bit of a purist when it comes to working out. I think it should involve a score. Running, jogging, stairing, lifting. No, no, no, no. That's why I like hockey: you drop your gloves and beat the shit out of them right there. They've got a special box where they make you sit for a couple of minutes, have a rest, a drink of water, and then you come back out whenever you're ready. I think that's a great idea. I think we should combine that with real life. I think everybody should have a penalty box at their jobs. You don't like your boss? Beat the shit out of him—take a five-minute penalty. People would be showing up to work at five o'clock in the morning: "I'm gonna hip-check you into the Xerox machine! I hate you!"

I'm a purist when it comes to all athletic activity. Figure skating? Hey. Either you dance or you skate. You don't do both. Get off the ice, okay? Go to a nightclub. Take off the skates.

Same with skiing. An Olympic sport? Moving down a hill? What's the scoreboard supposed to read? Mother Nature 12–You 7? No. The only interesting part of skiing is watching someone crash. Violently. Remember the guy from the beginning of ABC's "Wide World of Sports"? The Agony of Defeat guy? Now *that* is a sport. Come flying down the ramp and start bouncing down the mountain. If you live—you win. Medical Coverage 25–You 0.

That poor Agony of Defeat guy. One moment of his career—one mistake—played over and over and over again every Saturday on international TV. He must've walked around with a gun in his coat for years looking for Marshall McLuhan. *(Loading pistol)* "Global Village, my ass."

The Indians used to play a game that involved pushing a wooden hoop with sticks across vast territory. Across states. What we now know as Nebraska and Colorado and Wyoming. Of course, they hadn't divided the land so exactly so it probably didn't seem as far, but they would chase the hoop—tribes and tribes for miles and miles and miles. People would kill each other in the course of a game and a game would last for weeks.

That's what we need. Let's boil it down to the basic elements. Naked men with helmets and guns chasing each other across the open plain. Televise it. Throw in a couple of tanks and Humvees. "It looks like he's gonna make it—OH! He stepped on a land mine. That's gonna cost him."

Either that or let's allow drugs in all international athletic competition. Let's pump steroids and cocaine and testosterone—let's take actual testicles from donors and force-feed them to the athletes—let's inject them with Dexedrine and growth hormones—let's make the biggest, brawniest, most pissed-off, irritable edgy animals we can and then see how fast they can run—how high they can jump. Let's keep them in cages and launch them into enemy territory during the next war: "He's got Hussein in a headlock—OH! He's torn off Saddam's head!"

(Lights cigarette. Drags deeply. Inhales. Chugs beer. Exhales.)

I have the solution to the drug problem. Nobody asked me for it but here it is: not *less* drugs—*more* drugs. Get more drugs and give 'em to the right people. Because every time you read about some famous guy overdosing on drugs, it's always some really talented guy. It's always like Len Bias or Janis Joplin or Jimi Hendrix or John Belushi, you know what I mean?

The people you want to overdose on drugs never would. Mötley Crüe would never overdose! You could put them in a room with two tons of crack and they would come out a half hour later screaming, "Rock on!"

"Shit, they're still alive."

Unfortunately bands like the Crüe and the New Kids on the Block would never overdose.

I take music pretty seriously. *(Pulling up left sleeve)* You see that scar on my wrist? Do you know what that's from? I heard the Bee Gees were getting back together again. I couldn't take it, okay? That was the only good thing about the eighties—we got rid of one of the Bee Gees. One down, three to go. That's what I say, folks. Here's ten bucks, bring me the head of Barry Manilow. I want to drink beer out of his empty head. I want to have a Barry Manilow skull-keg party in my apartment, okay? You write the songs, we'll drink the beer out of your head. Barry Manilow—that's the U.S. contribution to world culture? You know how he made it? Overweight Catholic girls love Barry. He had a record-signing party in New York last year; there were one thousand overweight Catholic girls outside the record store going, "We love Barry Manilow. He's so cute. He's so sweet. I just want to meet him because I know he'll fall in love with me like I fell in love with him."

We live in the country where John Lennon takes six bullets in the chest and Yoko Ono—who's standing *right* next to him—doesn't get one bullet. Explain that to me, God. *(Banging on the floor)* I want it explained to me now! Now we've got twenty-five more years of "Yayaya-yayayayayaya!" I'm real happy, God. I'm wearing a huge happy hat. Jesus, give me a sign about this one.

Stevie Ray Vaughn is dead and we can't get Milli Vanilli on a helicopter? C'mon, folks. "Get on the 'copter, boys. There's free gum. Get on the 'copter. Get on that 'copter, c'mon. Vic Morrow's in there. He's the one without the head. Get on the 'copter!!" One of the boys in Milli Vanilli tried to commit suicide. I guess he finally listened to the album, huh?

What was that thing about heavy metal bands on trial a couple of years ago because kids were committing suicide? Judas Priest was on trial because *(whining)* "My kid bought the record and he listened to the lyrics and then he got into Satan and blah blah blah blah!" Well, that's great. That sets a legal precedent. Does that mean I can sue Dan Fogelberg for making me into a pussy in the mid-seventies? Is that possible? "Your honor, between him and James Taylor, I didn't have oral sex until I was thirty-one years old. I was in Colorado, wearing hiking boots and eating granola. I want some money right now."

Let me make sure I'm crystal clear on this issue. Heavy metal fans are buying heavy metal records, taking the records home, listening to the records and then blowing their heads off with shotguns? Where's the problem? That's an unemployment solution right there. It's called natural selection. It's the bottom of the food chain. Okay?

I don't go for this whole new thing that's happening to rock 'n' roll. You know, this new MTV movement with these new bands that are trying to start a late sixties, early seventies retro thing again? Bands wearing bell-bottoms again? No. Trying to start a sixties revival? No. Oliver Stone is the leader of this trend, isn't he? Every movie he makes is mired in the sixties. He made a two-hour movie about the Doors. Do we *need* a two-hour movie about the Doors? No. I can sum it up for you in five seconds: I'm drunk; I'm nobody. I'm drunk; I'm famous. I'm drunk; I'm dead. There's the whole movie. Okay? *Big Fat Dead Guy in a Bathtub.* There's the title for you! "It seems like an awful short script, Oliver. I don't know if we can shoot this or not."

(Lights up cigarette. Inhales. Exhales.)

And what about these rock bands that don't want to just be bands anymore? It's not enough to have a pop song that becomes a hit, or a dance number that people like to dance to. They want to be more than that. They want to tell us how to vote and how to feel about the environment. You know what I'm talking about? Like R.E.M. *(Singing)* "Shiny happy people . . ." "Hey, pull that bus over to the side of the Pretentiousness Turn-pike, all right? I want everybody off the bus. I want the shiny people over here and the happy people over here. I represent angry-gun-toting-meat-eating people, okay? So sit down and shut up!"

I got two words for Michael Stipe: Stevie Tyler. Okay? Don Henley's gonna tell people how to feel about the environment? I don't think so. A former member of the Eagles? I don't think so. I've got two words for Don Henley: Joe Walsh. Okay? Take off your ponytail and prepare to die. All right, Donny boy?

They should have shot all rock stars after Lennon was killed. They should have lined them up; we should have

47

gotten on the Partridge Family bus and driven around shooting them one by one.

Elvis Presley should have been shot in the head back in 1957 at close range with a .44 magnum. Just plant it right behind his brain stem. Sneak up from behind while he's sucking down a bowl of potatoes and BLAM! So you could remember him in a nice way. Wouldn't it be nice to remember Elvis thin with a big head of hair and that gold lamé suit? Wouldn't that have been nice? Sure it would. Because how do you remember Elvis? You know how you remember Elvis. He was found in the toilet with his pants around his ankles and his big, fat, hairy, sweaty, king of rock 'n' roll ass exposed to the world and his final piece of kingly evidence floating in the toilet behind him. Creepy! One of his aides had to walk in and go, "Dang, Elvis is dead. I better flush the toilet. *(Flush)* Oh, man, I should have saved that. I could have made some money off of that. Dang! Ding dang!" That's how you knew one of Elvis's guys was pissed, when he said "Ding dang!" instead of "Dang!"

So I'm glad Jesus died when he did. You know, if he'd lived to be forty he would have ended up like Elvis. C'mon. He had that big entourage—twelve guys willing to do anything he wanted to do. He was already famous at that point. If he had lived to be forty, he'd be walking around Jerusalem with a big fat beer gut and big black sideburns going, "Damn, I'm the son of God—give me a cheeseburger and french fries." "But, Lord, you're overweight." "Fuck you. I'll turn you into a leper. Now give me a cheeseburger and fries right now. Where's Mary Magdalene? I'm gettin' horny now. C'mon now."

I'm going to hell for that bit—and you're all coming with me! Don't try to get out of it. "We didn't laugh at that joke. Please, Jesus. Please don't make us go to hell."

"Get on the bus with Leary and Scorsese. You're goin' right to hell! Say 'Hi' to Andy Gibb for me when you get there." That's what hell is, folks. It's Andy Gibb singing "Shadow Dancing" for eons and eons. "Oh, my God. He's singing it again." And you have to wear huge bell-bottoms with orange polka dots and Hitler has all the coke.

Jesus was a great guy. He must have been incredibly patient. He didn't know he was the son of God until he was in his twenties, so as a teenager he had these incredible powers. And he never abused them. Not once. Not like you and I would. Oh, come on. If I had those powers at age seventeen, I'd be walking on water backward—naked—with a thirteen-inch erection—at the CYO picnic. *(Walking backward)* "Hey, girls! Look at this! Free wine for everybody!"

Jesus carried his cross through the streets for miles—with people spitting on his face. At the end of the journey they stripped him down and nailed him up. They stuck a lance in his side. Wow. I get tired carrying a bag of groceries two blocks. *(Out of breath)* "Shit . . . I shoulda had these delivered."

I'm sure he must be real happy about that Easter thing. He hangs on a piece of wood in the desert—hands and feet bleeding—he gives his life for our sins. Then three days later he comes back from the dead to forgive us. And how do we celebrate? By eating chocolate eggs. Yeah. Great. *(Hanging on the cross)* "Eggs, huh? Yeah, that's just fine. Why don't you get a bunny involved while you're at it? And some of those little pink marshmallow candies. Sure. Why not have a parade? Get some really expensive hats, hide the chocolate eggs and then look for them. What a tribute. Me? I'm fine. One of the great things about being a human is that you go into shock about half an hour into the agony. Get me something to drink, will ya? Sure—vinegar would be great. Just throw some vinegar on a rag and stick it into my mouth."

You would be hard pressed to get Jesus' name across in any of the messages we send to kids at Easter or Christmas. It's all eggs and bunnies and presents and reindeer. It's great when you're a kid. Until you hit the end of that first decade. When you're eight or nine or ten years old. When your parents tell you the truth. What a brick wall to run into, huh? Everything's going great and then one day—"Oh, by the way. Santa Claus and the Easter Bunny don't exist. The Tooth Fairy? Bullshit. And Big Bird isn't even remotely funny. Okay? Life's pretty good until you hit twenty-one, and then it's taxes and student payments and death and disease—if you live long enough to actually get one. Okay? Now run outside and play. And don't get hit by a car. We want you to live at least long enough to feel guilty about all the money we spent on the presents."

If Jesus came back now, he'd have to do a tour. A rock tour. Get a band together. The Apostles. Do a video. Get it in heavy rotation on MTV. Just to get his message across. And it would have to be a great show. All the promoters are complaining about high ticket prices and unsatisfied customers. It would have to be an outstanding show. *(High)* "Saw Jesus and the Apostles. Excellent, man. He played for three hours. Fed us all—bread, fish, wine. It was unfuckingbelievable. And for the encore? Awesome. He brought Jimi Hendrix back from the grave—Buddy Holly, Big Bopper, Janis, Lennon—and they did this all-star jam thing—they did a twenty-minute cover of 'Stairway to Heaven.' I almost puked—it was that intense."

I saw the Pope on his last American tour. I love the Pope. I think he's the best Pope we ever had—John Paul

George—the Beatle Pope. And he was such a regular guy. When you're the Pope, you can wear that ten-gallon Pope hat whenever you want to wear it. It's up to you—you are the Pope. But when he came to America on that big tour he didn't wear the giant Pope hat. He wore the tiny little Pope beanie. I admire that. He's trying to send a common-man image. I like a Pope who steps off the plane wearing a pair of Zebra jams and a White Sox cap—sucking down a Budweiser. *(Waving beer)* "God bless ya! What time's the show start? Let's rock!" *(Makes sign of the cross with beer can)*

Opening night for the Pope at his gig in Los Angeles was this Mexican kid. You must have seen the highlights on CNN. This kid was born with no arms. He taught himself how to play the guitar with his feet. The triumph of human nature. I was watching it on TV—he's playing some old spiritual—I can't even remember the song, I was so taken aback—he's taking solos—his toes are moving up and down the frets. And I just thought, "Man, what a miracle. This kid's born with no arms and now he's playing the guitar with his feet!" I couldn't play the guitar that well if I had been born with *ten* arms. But then again—I can blow my nose if I have to. God giveth and He taketh, you know what I'm saying? I'm sure the Pope found out pretty quick backstage after the show. "That was truly inspirational, Julio." "Thanks a lot. Hey, could you grab a Kleenex for me? I got a booger in my left nostril that's been whistling all night."

(Chugs more beer. Inhales deeply. Exhales with a loud spitting sound.)

I'm sick of these new rock stars. I'm fed up with the health kick rock 'n' roll's been on for the last decade. Bruce Springsteen, Madonna and even Mick Jagger.

They're all pumped up and worked out—Jagger's jogging fifteen miles a day. I like my rock stars the old-fashioned way. Skin and bones. Wasted away from drugs and drink. Tortured by their working-class origins and the wretched battle with early success. Open sores on their arms and scabs on their necks. Bad teeth. Bad sleep. Big chip on the left shoulder. The most exercise I want my rock stars to get every morning is when they pull the vomit out of their throats from the night before. *(Choking and pulling something out of mouth)* "Uh . . . oh—pizza!" *(Places it back in mouth)* "Tastes even better the second time around."

I shouldn't even mention Madonna in the same breath with rock 'n' roll. Or Cher. This is a whole different genre. Rock slash pop slash movie star slash disco diva slash, buy me some old riffs with new lyrics aerobicizers. Cher has a perfume, a workout tape and a diet book on the market. I saw her on TV pushing the sugar substitute Equal. She said—and I quote—"You care more about what you put in your car than you do about what you put in your body." Thanks, Cher. But I never put silicone breast implants in my car. And I never blew Sonny Bono, either. Two words: Gregg Allman. Okay?

I went to see Jerry Lee Lewis in concert last year. Unbelievable. Sixty-something years old and he played for two and a half hours without a break. And he's been married twenty times. He gets married on a Tuesday, they find his wife dead in a swimming pool on Thursday. The cops show up: "What happened, Jerry?" *(Shrugging)* "Ah dunno. Guess she drowned." Maybe if you married someone who's old enough to swim next time, okay, Jerry? Maybe that's the problem. Between you and Bill Wyman, there aren't any fourteen-year-olds left.

Bill Wyman's leaving the Rolling Stones. He's unhappy. Jesus, what does it take? Millions of dollars. Hundreds of millions of dollars. I read his book and he claims to have slept with five thousand women. Hey, Bill. I got news for you. You leave the band—it's over. You think you were getting laid off your looks or your dynamic onstage persona? Yeah, right. You were getting the women who couldn't get to Mick or Keith. Or Ron or Charlie. Or Brian Jones for that matter. *(Disappointed girl)* "You're sure he's really dead? Shit. And you can't dig him up? Guess I'll have to sleep with the bass player again."

Count your blessings, Bill. Morley Safer could get laid if he was the bass player for the Stones. Leonid Brezhnev. Richard Nixon. Quasimodo. Wake up and smell the set list, pal.

I thought rap was going to kick rock's ass with some street credibility, some gritty blood-soaked footsteps. NWA was at the top of the charts. Run DMC. Then. BANG! Vanilla Ice. Elvis Presley all over again. Colonel Tom Parker must've been sitting in his suite in Vegas going, "Get me a nahce young whaht boy ta sing this nigger music an' all them little whaht suburban girls'll be shakin' their little titties at 'im."

Vanilla Ice. If I was a black urban rap guy I would've been on a roof with a box of Tech 10s shooting every white pumps and red sweatpants. "There he is!" BLAM! "No—*there* he is!" BLAM!

Just like everything else, rap has been eaten up and poured into the mainstream. McDonald's commercials have rap beats. Everybody's rapping. Comedians. Morning FM radio zoos. The Pillsbury Doughboy is doing a rap commercial. Every time you turn on the TV it's "Ba dumpth—thump-dumpth—Ba-dumpth-thum-dumpth."

My dog is rapping: "B-b-ba-ba-bow wow. B-b-ba-bow wow." The cat's in the other room scratching. *(Running fingernails down box)* "Reow-reow-reow-reow." I don't want to see my dog rapping, okay? I'm pretty sure that's a sign of the apocalypse. "Honey—start the car. The dog is rapping."

I was reading a magazine recently with a Keith Richards interview in it. I'm flipping through because I like Keith and in the interview Keith Richards intimates that kids should *not* do drugs. But, Keith, we *can't* do any more drugs because you already did them all. There's none left. We have to wait till you die and smoke your ashes.

Of all the people to come down off the antidrug mountain and give us a seminar, Keith Richards—a guy with his own private blood and heroin supply. I don't think so. People marvel at Keith. "Hey, man. He did hard drugs and drinking for the last thirty-five years and I saw the last Stones tour and he looks pretty good." "Pretty good" is a relative term when it comes to Keith. It's one of those "pretty goods" you apply to a friend who's been through chemotherapy for the last six months and has just begun seeing visitors. You thought he was gonna be dead, but instead he just lost 125 pounds and has two hairs left on his head. "Well . . . I *guess* he looks pretty good . . . I mean, considering . . ." Take a good look at a photograph of Keith Richards's face. He's turned into leather. He's a giant suitcase. He has a handle on his head. That's how they move him around at the concerts. *(Lifting Keith up)* "Stand over here, Keith. No, stand over here. No . . ." He's got entire cities of miniature people driving around in those crevices on his cheeks. *(Waving)* "We get into the concerts for free!"

See, the rock stars told us to do the drugs back in the

sixties and the seventies, so now they feel guilty. "Do the drugs. Wear the bell-bottoms—we are! Stare at the album covers, there's messages in there!" Now they're trying to tell us to get off because they've quit. Hey, I don't need 'em to tell me. I quit it all, folks. I quit it all.

SMOKE

All I've got left are cigarettes and beer. That's it. That's all I have. *(Places lit cigarette on end next to bottle of beer)* These are my friends. Him and him. That's it. What more do you need, when you think about it? *(Indicating beer)* He's great. I love him. He's hops. He's barley. He's protein. He's a meal. But he's nothing without him *(indicating cigarette)*. It's one of him and one of him. Two of him and two of him. A carton of him and a case of him. Maybe their cousin Coffee comes over on the weekends for a visit. And I love the coffee and I love the beer —but I love you *(indicating cigarettes)* most of all. *(Picking up cigarette and carrying it around stage like a torch while dancing and singing)* I love you, I love you! I love to smoke, I'm singing the smoking song!

(Stops. Inhales. Exhales loudly. Inhales. Exhales loudly. Inhales three times quickly. Exhales a loud, long stream of smoke.)

I love to smoke. I smoke 7000 packs a day. Okay? I am never quitting. I don't care how many laws they make. What's the law now? You can only smoke in your apartment, under your blanket, with all the lights out? Is that the rule now? The cops are outside: "We know you have the cigarettes. Come out of the house with the cigarettes above your head." "You'll never get me, copper. I'm not comin' out, see! I've got a cigarette machine right here in my bedroom."

I'm sick and tired of these speeches from the non-smokers. *(Whining)* "That cigarette smoking is all psychological. Yes. That cigarette's just a replacement. You suck on that cigarette because you didn't suck on your mom long enough when you were a kid." That's the absolute truth. If I could buy a pack of breasts, I would. I'd be smoking forty to fifty packs a day. I'd never get out of the house. *(Leaning backward and sucking the nipple of a huge imaginary breast)* "Num num num num num num!" I'd be down the newsstand first thing every morning: "Gimme a pack of 44 Ds. You can leave the nipples on 'em."

I love to smoke. In fact I love to smoke so much that I'm gonna get a tracheotomy so I can smoke two cigarettes at the same time. *(Rapidly alternates inhaling cigarette through mouth and imaginary hole in neck)* I'm gonna get nine tracheotomies all the way around my neck. I'll be Tracheotomy Man. "He can smoke a pack at a time. He's Tracheotomy Man."

(Tosses cigarette onto stage and steps on it. Glances down. Steps on it again. Pauses. Slams foot over and over again onto cigarette butt.)

Gotta make sure it's out. Otherwise you get that toe cancer.

(Lights up new cigarette. Inhales. Exhales loudly, making the sound of a crazed elephant.)

I'm looking forward to cancer. I want that throat cancer. That's the best kind. You know why? Because when you get throat cancer you get a voice box. You know what I'm talking about? *(Speaking through a voice box— a distorted monotone)* The thing that *makes you talk like this.* Sure, it's scary but you can make money with a voice box. Get a voice box and walk around the streets of the city: *"Got any spare change?"* "Here's my whole wallet. Get away from me! AHHH!"

Can you imagine a whole family with voice boxes? That would be creepy, wouldn't it? They'd be out in the backyard every day during the summer:

"Dad can we go to the beach?"

"Yes. Get your mother and the dog. We'll leave right now."

"Sparky, come here."

"Arf. Arf arf arf."

But the ultimate irony is the guy with a voice box pulling up to the drive-through window at McDonald's. That has to suck, huh?

"Can I help you?"

"A Big Mac and a large order of fries."

"Stop making fun of me."

"I'm not making fun of you."

"Fuck you."

"Fuck you."

"I'm getting the manager."

"Get the manager. I don't care."

(Inhales deeply. Standing on one foot, he leans forward and spreads his arms in flight—like a fountain statue. He freezes for a moment.)

All the great Americans smoke. All the great Americans had cancer. John Wayne had cancer twice. The second time they took out one of his lungs he said, "Take 'em both out. I don't need 'em. I'll grow gills and breathe like a fish."

Babe Ruth was the greatest baseball player to ever play the game. He had a voice box. He was the first American to have a voice box. He had throat cancer for the last five years of his life and never complained once. "This is Babe Ruth, the Bambino, the Sultan of SWAT. I smoked twenty-five goddamn black Cuban cigars a day. I had meat for breakfast, lunch and dinner. I drank beer all day every day of my life. I fucked eighteen prostitutes *a night. And now I'm dead. Of course I'm dead—been dead for years. I'm up here in heaven. Lou Gehrig's up here with me. God love him. Lou Gehrig. Poor Lou Gehrig. Died of Lou Gehrig's disease. How the hell do you not see that coming? We even told him, 'Lou, there's a disease with your name all over it, pal!'"*

I don't know. *(Raises beer up in toast)* I think Billy Martin said it best when he said, "Hey—I can drive." *(Chugs beer)*

(Struts in a jaunty two-step across the stage, inhaling and exhaling to the beat of his feet. Tosses cigarette over shoulder, kicks it up in the air with right foot, turns and steps on it as soon as it lands on the stage. Lights a new cigarette. Inhales deeply. Exhales directly into front row.)

By the way, if you don't smoke—you might as well light up right now, because I'm gonna smoke so much during this show, you're gonna have cancer before you leave the building. You'll be walking out of the show going, "Great show. What's this thing on my neck?"

I love everything about smoking. I love the lighters, the ashtrays, the boxes the cigarettes come in. I love the little holes you burn in your clothing. But you know what I love most of all? The chest pains. Oh, the chest pains. Wake up in the morning after a big night of smoking: *(Staggering and clutching chest)* "Omigod. Omigod! I'm having a heart attack! OMIGOD! Why did I smoke? Why did I—(Pauses, feeling better)* Oh. They're gone. Light up another cigarette. I better hurry up. I got some more chest pains coming in about five minutes."

I tried quitting. I got one of those nicotine patches in my arm. It releases small doses of nicotine into your system every ten minutes. I got the patch and had a big box of nicotine gum. I lit up. WOW! Best high I ever had.

(Inhales. Tries to exhale but no smoke comes out. Punches himself in the heart and—finally—exhales.)

They say every cigarette takes three minutes off your life. So a pack would be sixty minutes, a carton would be . . . I don't think I'm gonna make it through the show.

(Stamps out cigarette in ashtray. Puts four new ones into mouth. Lights up. Inhales. Exhales a huge thick cloud of smoke.)

There goes another twelve minutes.

I wouldn't quit smoking tomorrow if they found a tumor the size of my head in the middle of my chest. You know why? Because nonsmokers have too much power now. They have their own lobbying groups, they have their own pamphlets, they have their own advertisements. Have you seen the famous dead celebrity ads? They get a celebrity who's dying from a cigarette-related disease and they film a commercial with him just before he kicks the bucket—then they run the commercial to make us feel creepy and queasy. John Huston did one. John Huston died when he was almost ninety years old. Now they have this shot of him in a wheelchair, with an oxygen tank and a mask over his face going *(raspy, struggling-for-breath voice),* "Whoo-huhh. This is John Huston. Whoo-huhh. Don't smoke. Whoo-huhh. I'm warning you! Whoo-huhh. Don't smoke! Whoo-huhh. God, I wish I could have a cigarette. Whoo-huh. Please get me a cigarette. Whoo-huhh." I'm sitting at home watching it on TV going, "Man, I wish I had that kind of setup. I could get up to ten thousand packs a day."

There's a group of you nonsmokers I admire. There's a group of you nonsmokers that I love. The ex-smokers. The ones who used to smoke. I love you—'cause you leave more cigarettes for me. And you have something I don't have. Will power. Yes. I never had will power about smoking. I never had the word "quit" pop into my head about smoking ever. Not for a second. Not for a millisecond.

And it's always the same story, isn't it? Doesn't matter how long you smoked—seven days, seven minutes, seven months, seven years, seven decades. Doesn't matter how long you've quit—a week, a month, a year, twelve years, twelve hundred years! It's always the same feeling, isn't it? You feel good most of the time. But you have those little humps, don't you? Those little speed bumps that pop up out of nowhere—BANG BANG—and drop you to your knees begging for nicotine. *(Walking proudly)* "Haven't had a cigarette in ten years! Lips that touch tobacco will never touch mine!" *(Stops. A loud snapping sound as his head twists to the side. Drops to his knees, suddenly crying and pleading.)* GIMME A CIGARETTE! PLEASE! I'LL DO ANYTHING! PLEASE! I'LL BLOW YOU! I'LL CLEAN YOUR TOILETS! PLEASE! GIMME ONE. *(Stops. A loud snapping sound is heard as his neck returns to its original position. He stands and walks away, strutting proudly.)* Haven't had a cigarette in ten years, two weeks, three days, four hours and—*(checking watch)* forty-two minutes, fifteen seconds!

Yet sometimes when you're at work and you're sitting at your desk, someone a few cubicles away lights up. And you can smell it—SNIFF! It's getting closer—SNIFF! Now you want one—SNIFF! You're going to march over and stab that smoker in the balls and take his pack and light them all up at once and suck in and blow out HAH-

HAH! FUCK YOUR LUNGS FUCK CANCER FUCK THE WORLD I WANNA SMOKE GODDAMMIT! But you stop yourself. You sit down. You breathe deeply. You put one of your tapes—the sound of waves or wind or synthesized violins—into your Walkman, and you listen and you calm down and you feel better. You think of how long you'll live. You think of all the money you'll save. You think of all the money you spend on those New Age therapeutic tapes. And you realize you couldn't afford to smoke even if you wanted to.

So you don't have one. And you feel better. Will power. Yeah.

Maybe you invite some friends over to the house and they smoke. You let them smoke in the house and they smoke and they drink and they smoke and they eat and they smoke and they have another drink and they go home. Now you can see the smoke. SNIFF. It's in the kitchen. SNIFF. It's in the hallway. SNIFF. It's in the bathroom. SNIFF. It's everywhere. SNIFF SNIFF. It's taking over the apartment. SNIFF SNIFF SNIFF. You can reach out and taste it. You want one desperately. You'd sell both your kidneys for just one cigarette. AHH-HHHH. But you don't have one. You just empty the ash-trays and you go to bed without smoking and you feel good about yourself. God bless you. Will power. Yeah.

(Pauses. Inhales deeply on four cigarettes. Stubs them out in ashtray. Exhales. Picks up pack. Plucks a cigarette from it and lights up. Inhales. Smiles. Exhales. Takes another cigarette from pack. Admires it. Holds it aloft.)

But it's a little bit different story when one just *(tosses unlit cigarette into audience)* DROPS in your lap! That's a hell of a difference, isn't it? *(Tosses another cigarette into the audience)* Let's talk about will power now, folks. C'mon. Let's discuss will power. *(Tosses another cigarette)* Let's dissect will power. *(Tosses another)* C'mon. *(Tosses another)* Will power. Will power. *(Tosses several at once)* Just a couple of words placed together. Will. Power. C'mon. Light up. LIGHT UP! *(Tosses a handful)* GIVE IN! *(Tosses remainder of pack)* Stop fighting the urge. Give in. Enjoy. Relax. *(Tosses empty pack)*

(Mimicking audience) "Oh, please, Mr. Leary. Please don't make us smoke. Please? Smoking takes ten years off your life." Well, it's the ten worst years, isn't it? It's the ones at the end! It's the wheelchair-kidney-dialysis-adult-diaper years. I don't want them. I'll tell you one thing. If I live that long, I'll still be smoking. I'll be in my wheelchair with my adult diapers on, hooked up to my machines. My thirty-four-year-old nonsmoking son will be standing behind me. I'll be going, "Change my diaper. And make sure you wipe this time. My ass was itching all week. And get me another lighter."

We tried to be nice to you nonsmokers. We tried. You wanted your own sections in restaurants; we gave that to you. But that's not enough for you, is it? Because every smoker here knows that when you sit in the "Smoking Area," the legal little area where you're allowed to smoke, and you screw that baby onto your lips and you light it up—and you taste your first few relaxing sucks— "Ahh . . . Ahh . . ."—what do you hear coming from that nonsmoking section? Those little pussy-coughs: "Ahem . . . Ahem . . . AHEM . . . ACHH! . . . ACHH! . . . AHHCHCHCH! . . . THE SMELL OF YOUR CIGARETTE IS KILLING ME!"

Oh? It's the smell of my cigarette—it's not the smell of urine in New York—it's my cigarette? You wanted the airplanes? We gave you the whole goddamned plane. Are you happy now? I'd like an explanation about that one, folks, because I'll guarantee you that if the plane is going down the first announcement you're going to hear is: "Folks, this is your captain speaking. Light 'em up because we're goin' down. Okay? I've got a carton of Camel unfiltereds. I'll see ya on the ground. Take it easy." Actually, it's more like this *(through a voice box): "This is your captain speaking. Smoke 'em if you got 'em."*

And you're always doing your nonsmoking math, aren't you? Always figuring out the future. "Okay. I'm thirty-four. If I quit smoking now, I'll live to be . . . about seventy. . . . Okay, I'm thirty-seven . . . if I quit now I'll live to be . . ." Forget it. Forget it all. Stop trying to seal your fate. You quit. And then you start jogging and stairing and lifting and eating high fiber and drinking carrot juice and planning for the future. HEY! Two words: Jim Fixx. Remember Jim Fixx? The jogging guru? Wrote a jogging book, did a jogging video and dropped dead of a massive heart attack. When? When he was jogging, that's when. What do you want to bet it was two smokers who found the body the next morning? *(Inhaling, staring at the ground)* "Hey. That's Jim Fixx, isn't it? What a tragedy. C'mon. Let's go buy some cigarettes." *(Dances joyfully away, inhaling and exhaling with loud, rhythmic popping sounds)*

It's always the nonsmoking, sprout-eating yogurt-shake-sucking high-fiber eaters who get run over by a bus driven by a fat guy who smokes three packs a day. *(Leaning out window of bus)* "Sorry, Officer. Didn't even see him. I was too busy smoking." *(Drives off, smoking and beeping horn)*

I want an iron lung. I want an iron lung in my house. I want an iron lung right in the middle of my apartment. I want to lie in it. On my back. On my back with a little reflecting mirror I can look into and see my favorite shows on TV. I want an electric wheelchair. I want an electric wheelchair with one of those bite mechanisms. You just bite into it and steer yourself around the house. I want to bite down and drive into the kitchen and say: "Honey? Could you light me a smoke and stick it into my lips? Oh, by the way. My colostomy bag is full."

Your parents smoked. Your grandparents smoked. Your great-grandparents smoked. Your parents smoked and ate bad food and drank. Your parents had heart attacks all the time. Your father would clutch his chest, bend over in pain and ride it out. Then he'd stand up, suck down a piping-hot cup of black coffee and go to work. Your mother found a tumor in her neck, she'd lance it off and throw it in with the brussels sprouts for dinner. "Ma—this one tastes kinda funny." "Shut up and eat it. It's good for ya!"

JFK smoked. Lee Harvey Oswald didn't. John Lennon smoked. Mark David Chapman didn't. The Rolling Stones smoked. The Bee Gees didn't. Winston Churchill smoked. Hitler didn't. And Hitler was a vegetarian. I rest my case.

Smokers don't snap. We don't suddenly hop into a pickup truck, drive downtown and strafe the sidewalk with an automatic rifle. We think about it. We sit down, light up and think about it over a cup of coffee. But we don't have time to kill other people. We're too busy killing ourselves. "Well, I'd sure like to drive into that restaurant across the street, line up all the nonsmokers and shoot their brains out. But then I'd have to go to prison. And cigarettes are hard to get in prison."

Wouldn't it suck for you nonsmokers if you got up to the pearly gates—all those years of wondering and sweating and praying and hoping—and St. Peter calls out your name and you step forward and he says, "Welcome to heaven. Got a light?"

It's always sad when nonsmokers die from a heart attack, isn't it? Yeah, it is. Because you know the first thing they're thinking is "Damn! I could've smoked! I could have shot heroin right into my neck, for crissakes! Why was I such a health nut? Now I'm dead!"

Don't smoke in cabs. Wait a minute. We can't smoke in cabs because the driver is so concerned about his health. As he careens through the city streets at 7000 miles an hour. *(Flying all over the back of a cab at high speeds)* "Look out! Jesus! There's a truck! Holy shit! Watch for that bike guy! Phew! Good thing I'm not smoking, huh?"

You want one, don't you? Your fingers are twitching and so are your lungs. You're thinking, "Denis, does it still taste as good as it used to?" Guess what? It tastes better.

(Inhales deeply. Exhales. As the smoke wafts up into the lights, he grabs a handful and rubs it all over his body. He reaches up daintily and with his pinky finger takes a dab of smoke and places it behind each ear. Inhales deeply again. Exhales. The smoke once again wafts up into the lights. He sucks it all back into his mouth. He swallows it.)

I love to smoke and I love to smoke and I love to smoke and I love to eat red meat. I love to eat raw red meat. There's nothing I like better than to suck down a hot steaming butt and eat a raw cheeseburger at the same time. I love to smoke and I love to eat red meat and I only eat red meat that comes from cows that smoke. They're special cows they grow in Virginia with voice boxes in their necks. *(Through voice box)* "Mooooo."

I tried eating vegetarian. But I felt like a wimp going into a restaurant: "What do you want to eat, sir?"

"Broccoli." Hey, broccoli is a side dish, folks, always was, always will be, okay? When they ask me what I want, I say, "What do you think I want? This is America; I want a bowl of red meat. Forget about that! Bring me a live cow over to the table! I'll carve off what I want and ride the rest home." *(Rides cow across the stage while singing the theme song from "Bonanza")* People go, "Yeah, but you eat red meat and it stays in your colon for fifteen years." Good, I paid good money for it. I want them to find my colon wrapped in a meat sweater when they open me up in the end. "This guy's covered in meat. He's Meat Man! He's Meat-Tracheotomy Man!"

We have to eat the cows. If we don't eat the cows, they'll take over the whole planet. *We'll* be out in the fields naked, eating grass. You don't want that, now do you? "Hey, you guys. There's some really nice mulch over here."

People say, "Why do we eat cows?" I'll tell you why. Because we can, that's why. Because we are superior. Because we have guns and they don't.

I'm gonna open my own place and get away from you nonsmokers and vegetarians. That's what I'm gonna do. I'll open my own place with two smoking sections: "ultra" and "regular," okay? We're not gonna have any tables or any chairs or any napkins or any silverware, none of that stuff. Just a big wide-open black hole and all we're gonna serve is raw meat right on the bone! Only men are gonna eat there—naked men sitting by a big giant campfire. No men's room either; if you have to go to the bathroom you piss wherever you are and mark your territory like a wolf! If some guy has a heart attack from eating too much meat we'll throw him on the fire—more meat for the other meat eaters! Because you've got to have goals, folks.

Believe me, I know why you're quitting the meat. I know why you're quitting the meat and the booze and the smoking and everything else. I hear ya knockin'— well, come on in! You want to quit meat and smoking and everything because you want to live longer. Sure. You want to have more time to live so you have more time to save the planet. I understand. You want more time to spend with your loved ones. I understand—but what's the point? We've got about five years left on this planet, folks, war or no war. There's a giant hole in the ozone. We broke the sky. I think we should feel a little guilty about that. You read about it in the paper and go, "Geez, it's terrible what we're doing to the ozone." Then when it's 95 degrees in New York City the day after Christmas: "Well, it's not *that* bad. Honey, get a case of Right Guard and spray it right into the goddamned sky. Screw the environment, I'm going golfin' tomorrow."

Everybody has a friend who's quitting everything.

They love to tell you about it too. *(Puffing out chest and strutting across stage)* "I quit it all. I quit it all. I quit smoking. I quit booze; quit meat; quit drugs, and I feel *great*. I get up in the morning; eat a big bowl of oat bran. I go to the bathroom for three and a half hours. I have another bowl of oat bran and go back into the bathroom for six more hours. All I do is eat and shit! I'm gonna live forever! My colon is the strongest muscle in my body right now. I could pass Elvis through my colon right now! A quarter through my colon right now!"

All these cereals they have: Cracklin' Oat Bran, and Horkin Fiber Chunks. Cereal used to come with a free prize and now it comes with a roll of toilet paper in every box. Guys get up on Sunday morning and say, "Forget about the newspaper, I'm gonna read the Bible—I've got a big one brewin' here."

"Dad, there's a phone call."

"I'm on Genesis, goddammit. You tell them to call back after the creation."

You people checking your own feces for fiber—you have too much free time on your hands, okay? "Honey, I think there's some broccoli at this end. Isn't that nice?"

Oat bran. Every five years science comes up with some miracle solution. Some bookworm with a government grant locked up in a lab at M.I.T. with 700 mice finds a thread for his article in *Science Monthly* and all of a sudden everything has oat bran in it. They have mice in those labs who have eaten nothing but grape Jell-o for twenty-five years and show no signs of cancer. But they know we wouldn't buy the grape Jell-o theory. So they push the oat bran mouse. *(Studious, professional voice)* "Well, we fed this mouse nothing but oat bran for twenty-five years and not only is he cancer-free but his cholesterol is substantially lower."

Bang! We're all buying oat bran. Oat bran cereal. Oat

bran soap. Oat bran hats. All of a sudden every product has oat bran. And labels on the front screaming the bad things it doesn't contain. "No cholesterol!" "No sugar added!" "No feces!" *(Happy consumer voice)* "I'm getting those No Feces Flakes. They don't have any feces in them at all. The other flakes must be loaded with feces!"

Suck down some meat, folks. Do yourself a favor. Bite into it. Feel that protein coursing through your veins. It's the American Way. James Garner. Now there's a real American for you. He was advertising beef on TV, he had open-heart surgery and *kept* advertising beef on TV. Now there's a real man. "Hi. James Garner here. AH! *(Clutches chest in pain)* JESUS! *(Grabs left wrist)* SHIT! *(Clutches chest again)* MAN! *(The pain suddenly subsides and he recovers)* Phew. You know, I love beef. I can't get enough of it! AH! *(Clutches chest again)*."

Sting. When did Sting become Mr. Multifacet? He used to just be a pop singer. Now every time you see his name it's got all these other titles attached to it. Sting: pop singer slash poet slash jazz musician slash environmentalist. Jazz musician? I've got two words for Sting's ability to play jazz: my ass, okay? "Sixty Minutes" did a tribute to Sting. I thought that was reserved for artists who'd been around for a while and proven themselves—maybe they're seventy or eighty and they're going to die, so Morley Safer gives them a chance to sum up their contribution to society. Let Barbara Walters do the fluffy little pieces. No. Sting's on there and he is talking about jazz and the environment and I'm thinking, "This guy is either the most sensitive guy in the history of mankind or he's really desperate to get laid." They show this clip of Sting when he was on the Rain Forest Tour and Sting had taken this rain forest chief around the world to talk to reporters about the plight of his homeland. This guy's never been out of the rain forest. Now this chief is probably a pretty cool-looking guy *in* the rain forest. But once you pluck him out, he's got problems that go way beyond bell-bottoms. They show this clip of him and Sting at a press conference in L.A. and the chief has this giant ring implanted in his bottom lip, like a piece of metal or wood that makes his lip protrude a good five inches from his face. And I'm watching this and thinking, "Hey, looks like an ashtray to me. I'd love to go on tour with the chief."

"We're trying to raise money to help preserve the rain forest, and . . ." *(Flicking ashes into the lip)* "Oh, sorry. Did I burn you? Well, get Sting to buy you a new lip with some of his rain forest money."

And how about these people who are eating placenta? Have you heard about these people? Folks, these people have driven down to the end of the Nature Turnpike, okay? They're the ones who are having babies, saving the placenta in Tupperware, bringing it home, making placenta cakes, and eating them! They think you should eat placenta because that's what animals do. Well, animals also lick their own balls. Do we have to do *that* too?

I can't prove it, but I think Sting is behind this somehow. Sting. He wants to save the whales. He wants to save the seals. He wants to save the rain forest. Why doesn't he start by saving his own hair?

When did Sting become the rock-icon-spokesman for a generation? Do we really need rock stars to tell us how to feel about the environment?

I want to save the environment. I love the environment. Trees, rocks, dirt, I love all those things. Animals? I love animals. Being an animal lover is great—but some people take it a little bit too far.

Did you hear about the pit bull victim in England? It was on CNN. International news. England has this huge problem with pit bull breeding. England—the country where all you hear about is how violent America is and what a bunch of killers we are and how we should control our guns. When you enter England, the customs guy will ask you point-blank if you have any guns. No guns are allowed in England at all. The cops on the beat don't even carry guns. But pit bulls are allowed to run wild. "Are you bringing any firearms into the country?" "No, just this vicious, man-eating four-legged killing machine." "Oh. Well, go right ahead, sir."

So this English guy is walking home one night—all alone. And these two pit bulls attack him. Just jump him. And they knock him down and rip his face to shreds—tear off part of one ear, rip off his entire nose, tear up his lips. They rush him to the hospital and do seven hours of surgery. He decided to hold a press conference to show the world the damage the dogs have done. So he's sitting at a table on CNN with a bank of microphones in front of him and this torn-up face and no nose. They have to do a skin graft and several more operations to replace the nose. And he says—and I quote—"Despite my ordeal—" Oh. I can't actually do his voice because, well, I have a nose. Yeah. It's right here *(points to nose)*. So he says, "Despite my ordeal, I still love dogs." He still loves dogs! Some people never learn, do they? The pit bulls are ripping his face apart and he's going: "Good doggy. C'mere. You playful little thing. Here. *(Throws nose)* Go fetch my nose. Go fetch it. Bring it back to me! Goood dog. Have an ear, boy. Have an ear." Some people just never learn.

I have a dog. I love my dog. You guys have pets. You love your pets and they love you. You know why? Because you have the food. It's as simple as that.

We love to talk to our pets. "Come here, doggy. Come here. Sit. Give me the paw. Okay, roll over. Oh, look at him. He's so cute; he's almost human." There's the problem, right? We have these little cute pangs in our bellies because we're human beings. That's how we decide which animals to save. It's all a matter of how cute they are. *(Gazing longingly into distance)* "Oh, look at the baby seals with the big brown eyes and the furry little fur. Don't do anything to them. Leave them alone." *(Gazing off to the side with a healthy thirst)* "But the cows are big and dumb and stupid. Fuck them. Let's eat them all. C'mon. Let's make jackets out of what's left over. C'mon." We might as well just have animal auditions and line them up one by one and judge them individually.

"What are you?"

"I'm an otter."

"And what do you do?"

"I swim around on my back and do cute little human things with my hands."

"You're free to go." *(Gives the otter the thumbs-up sign, turns back)*

"And what are you?"

"I'm a cow."

"Get in the fuckin' truck, okay, pal?"

"But I'm an animal."

"You're a baseball glove."

"I'm an animal."

"You're a hat. Get on that truck. You cow. What do you think we called you a 'cow' for?"

We kill the cow to make jackets out of them, then we kill each other for the jackets that we made out of the cows. I think the cows would love that joke, don't you? *(As cow)* "They're killin' each other for their jackets? *Mooo.*"

I don't think it proves superior intelligence on our part that we can fashion a bat out of a piece of wood and bomp a baby seal over the head with it. Seals are very intelligent animals. They've probably thought of defending themselves. Only one problem: no hands. They're sitting on the beach, getting womped on the head, going: THONK "Man, this sucks." THONK "Wish we had some hands." THONK "Or at least a couple of helmets." THONK.

And let's be honest, folks. How many whales do we really need? I figure five. One for each ocean. We save their semen in a huge mayonnaise jar, we procreate them when we need to. The world is full of starving children, but every time a whale beaches himself we're spending billions of dollars to develop and build special equipment to unplug them and send them back out to sea. But maybe these are dysfunctional whales. Maybe they're *trying* to commit suicide. Maybe they don't want to go back out to sea. *(As whale)* "Leave me die, man. The other whales hate me. I'm sick of it all. I'm sick of the swimming and the spouting and trying to avoid fishing boats. C'mon. Harpoon me. Put me out of my misery. Put a few hundred pounds of coke in my blowhole and let me overdose."

Here's what sums up the animal rights movement to me. You've all heard this one, haven't you? *(Walking to lip of stage in tears)* "Don't eat the tuna fish." Why? *(Crying)* "Dolphins are getting stuck in the nets!" "But what about the tuna fish?" *(Recovering)* "Well, fuck them. They taste good. They never had their own TV show, for crissake. They never swam next to our boats and made cute little sounds. Get out of here, tuna fish. I'm gonna make a sandwich out of you. You cute little dolphin. Tuna fish never had their own football team. I love the little dolphin. *(Petting him)* I love the little Dan Marino dolphin, man."

(Chugs remainder of his beer. Pulls another from behind crate, opens it and takes a long slug. Lights up. Inhales. Exhales.)

You will eat the meat, folks. Believe me, you will eat the meat. I know there's a couple o' vegetarians out there. There's a couple in every crowd. Vegetarians are nice people. They're very nice people. They have their own food. Celery. Mmmm. Celery tastes good. For about fifteen minutes. Then they break out the potatoes. Every vegetarian I know has about a million ways to make potatoes. They love potatoes, don't they? *(Pleading)* "Hey, you wanna come over tomorrow night for dinner? We're having cheese and potatoes. You wanna come over? The night after that we're having Cajun potatoes. They're really good. You wanna come over? C'mon. Saturday night, we're having spaghetti and potatoes. You wanna come over? Huh? Please come over. Please come over and eat some potatoes. Please? We've got millions of potatoes. Please come over and eat some. Please?"

You will eat the meat. You will. Did you ever see the movie *Alive*, based on the book *Alive*, based on the true story? A rugby team flying over the Andes Mountains in an airplane. The plane crashes. Some of the players die. The others have to *eat* them to survive. Now I'm not saying this is gonna happen to you tomorrow. But—it's a possibility, isn't it? Let's say you're going on vacation. You're taking an airplane. *And* you're taking a friend with you? Just make sure it's a really fat guy. Fatten him up more before you go. "Have another burger, Bill. I just love to see you eat." Nothing worse than being stuck up in the Andes Mountains in a plane crash with your anorexic friend Freddy. "Have something to eat, Fred." "Naw, I had a raisin three weeks ago. I'm full." If you can't find a fat friend to travel with you, just make sure you sit next to a fat guy on the plane. *(Sitting down)* "He's all mine! Get away from him! *(To fat guy)* Anything you want to eat is on me. Here. Have a Twinkie."

Everybody is food. We forget that basic fact of life,

don't we? Every *thing* is food. Did you hear about the guy in the Philippine earthquake last year? Earthquake. Three days later, they are digging through the rubble—figuring everyone buried is dead now—they find a guy alive under the remains of a building. They pull the guy out and he looks pretty good. A couple of scratches, a few broken bones. They ask him, "How did you survive for three days?" He says, "I drank my own urine." Yikes. That is frightening, isn't it? A basic survival instinct bubbling below in our bones. A thought balloon that only appears in moments of extreme emergency. As a last resort. You're trapped under a fallen building. Wondering what to do. Suddenly an enzyme snaps into place and you think, "Ah! I'll drink my own urine." You pull out your penis—and strangely enough, right on the side, it says, "In case of emergency, point at mouth."

You could eat anybody or anything to survive. You think you won't but you will. You could eat your cat. Sure you could. Or your dog. Yes.

They are meat. So are you. Hypothetical situation: you are on a boat. With your dog. And your cat. It's a Sunday. You decided to take your pets on a pleasure cruise. Things are going great. You're laughing. You're singing. Suddenly you realize that you're way off course. You've lost sight of the shoreline. The engine's dead. You drift and drift, waiting for help. Days go by. You're starving. The dog is starving. The cat is starving. Guess who's down first. You got it. The cat. He's small, he's easier to kill and he was always kind of an independent little prick. Once you've eaten the cat, how hard would it be to eat the dog? Sure he's cuddly and loyal—but there's a lot more meat on a dog. See? Pets are great. For two reasons. They always hang around you, number one. *And* they're great food insurance in case of an emergency.

Always bring your dog—and bottle of ketchup—wherever you go.

You will eat the meat, folks, because it's a decision not to eat meat. It's an instinct to want it. You don't pop out of your mother's womb and go, "Yah, I'll have some soybean milk and some eggplant, please." No. You pop out of there and go, "I'll have some breast milk and a cheeseburger medium and cut this shit off before a placenta eater shows up." Because eggplant tastes like eggplant but meat tastes like murder and murder tastes pretty good, doesn't it? Yeah. You all had meat at Thanksgiving and Christmas, didn't you? I can smell it on you. The holidays are the meat seasons, aren't they? That's always been the way, hasn't it? Remember when you were a kid? Remember Christmastime when you were a kid? Your mom would cook that big roast beast. Remember that? Remember that big chunk of beef your mom would cook at Christmastime with all the blood in the bottom of the plate? Your dad would carve up the slices. *(Cutting meat with an electric knife)* Rrrr . . . Rrrrr . . . and you get a piece of meat and some vegetables and potatoes and your mom would pour the blood over the whole thing. You would suck it all down and then lick your bloody little fingers and then open up your presents. "Oh, thank you, Daddy, a train. Thank you, Daddy." *(Evil)* "MORE MEAT, DADDY!"

Meat is good. Meat is fun. Yea for meat. Give me an "M"!

This country was founded on meat. The Indians ate meat. The Pilgrims ate meat. And when the Pilgrims ran out of meat—they ate the Indians.

Meat is Mom. Meat is music. Meat is mystery. Yeah. Every cheeseburger you've ever eaten anywhere in the world always has that piece of gristle in it. You don't know what it is. *(Chewing)* "Could be a bone . . . could be a tooth . . . I don't care what it is but I'm eating it."

Meat. Red meat. White meat. Gray meat. Brown meat. Blue meat. Black meat. Gray meat with that little rainbow of weird greenish-orange colors in it. Meat stuck to bones. Meat juice. Meat candy. Meat-o-rama.

Do you understand democracy? Do you understand civilization? We pay good money to farmers who grow the meat. They send the meat to packing plants. The packing plants slaughter and crush the cows and pack the meat in boxes. They send the boxes to your local supermarket where big beefy men in white coats with cigarettes dangling from their lips stick it into cute little Styrofoam containers and high school kids cover it with plastic wrap. Don't you see? Everyone has a job, the kids are off the streets and you don't have to actually kill and skin the animal. You just go to the store and pick out your favorite package, buy it, bring it home and eat it. One two three. Simple. Beautiful. The way God meant it to be.

This country is even shaped like a giant flank steak. Florida is the bone sticking out of the bottom.

(Takes a long hard swig of beer. Sucks furiously on cigarette. Stubs it out. Lights up a fresh butt. Inhales. Exhales.)

This country was founded on two things: meat and war. They came together during the Persian Gulf crisis in my living room. You know how I watched that war break out? Naked in my living room with a can of Budweiser and a plate of meat with the war live on TV! I was walkin' around with a boner and a cheeseburger on the end goin', "Yeah! We kicked the shit out of a country the size of Rhode Island and I feel pretty good about it. Let's take Connecticut next, c'mon. Martha's Vineyard! Free cheeseburgers for everybody!" Vietnam vets must have been real happy about that war. They put in fifteen years of toil, sweat and blood. They come home and they're treated like shit. These guys are over there for fifteen minutes. They come home. There's victory parades and souvenir hats and TV specials. If I were a Vietnam vet, I would have been down at that victory parade with a pocketful of hand grenades and an Uzi just strafing the crowd. BLAM! BLAM! BLAM! BLAM! BLAM BLAM BLAM BLAM! "Hey! Whaddaya doing?" *(Searching for a way out)* "It's a flashback!" BLAM! BLAM! BLAM BLAM BLAM BLAM! "They *all* look like Kong to me." I'll tell you something. It's a stupid feeling but we've got to enjoy it while we can, okay? Because when was the last time we really kicked some ass in a war? A long time ago, so let's enjoy the feeling. Let's take advantage of it.

We have souvenir shops in airports where you can buy Persian Gulf hats and Schwarzkopf T-shirts and Fuck Saddam buttons. Where were the Vietnam souvenir shops? "Yeah. I'll have a land mine, two severed legs and a can of Agent Orange, please?"

We were hungry for a war, weren't we? We wanted that American macho image back, and we got it. We've been bummed out for years about our image. We invented the space shuttle. It was our weapon of the future. No one else had one. And then—tragedy. I think we all felt the same when the space shuttle blew up. I think we all thought the same thought when we found out it had exploded: "Damn! I forgot to set my VCR. Now I'm gonna have to borrow the tape."

We really think we're going to Mars. The government believes this. I love that line of logic. *(Official government voice)* "Don't worry about the ozone or cancer or AIDS. We ruined this planet. No problem. We'll just move to Mars." Yeah, right. And take all our problems with us. Get there. Build our bubble. Live under it for a few years and then: "Fuckin' antenna-heads. They get cable for free! Next thing you know, they'll wanna play baseball too."

Mars. Sure it would be hot. But you'd be able to light your cigarette right off the ground. *(Hops from foot to foot and bends down to press end of cigarette to stage)* Ahhh.

The thing that still sticks with me about the space shuttle explosion is the people who were there watching it go up live. The parents, the kids? Those poor kids. They had some of that teacher's students flown down for the gig. And these poor innocent kids are watching the thing go up, waving their little American flags. That was the saddest and at the same time funniest video I ever saw. *(Looking up, wide-eyed and innocent)* "There goes our teacher . . . yay . . . she's—hey, wait a minute . . . what the? . . . (crying)* WAHHHHHH!!" Scarred for life! Twenty years from now when another nut drives into McDonald's and shoots fifteen people and they wonder why? He'll tell you why. *(Brandishing a rifle, crazed)*

"Because I watched my teacher blow up on national TV . . . that's why!" BLAM! BLAM! BLAM BLAM BLAM!

Christa McAuliffe. First teacher in space? First teacher all over space. *(Looking up)* "There she is! No, *there* she is. No, *there* she is. THERE! THERE! THERE!"

But you find out who your friends are in time of war. We decided we were going into the Persian Gulf and England was right behind us, weren't they? *(Hopping about, excitedly)* "You guys going in? We're right behind you! Yup! Yup! Wouldn't miss it! You got those nuclear weapons, right? Great! Great. You got some air conditioners? Great! Let's go!"

England had Thatcher. We had Reagan. They were the best of friends. Two old battle horses just dying to get into a war. Stockpiling weapons and lining the pockets of their friends. But at least we have one thing we can hold over England's head. At least we tried to kill Reagan.

Reagan would have loved the Persian Gulf War. It was perfect. Bush tried to pass it off under the old agenda. "We're going to war over human rights and oppression." No. It was oil. If Kuwait's main export was white cotton socks we wouldn't have been so quick to anger, would we? *(Marching)* "We've gotta save those socks, man! Summertime's coming up!"

Most Americans didn't even know where Kuwait was until the war was over. That's the way we are in this country. First order of attack, we put on our million-dollar helmets and jump into our billion-dollar planes and go: "Kuwait? Where the hell is that?" "It's near Israel. Just fly around for a while and blow something up."

Of course we have to defend Kuwait. Because they have oil. And we deserve the most oil because we drive the biggest cars. I'm sick and tired of being told by other countries and some of our own senators that we ought to be driving smaller cars. We can't fit in the small cars. We're too fat from eating cheeseburgers and drinking beer and watching television all day. I'm not giving up big cars. That's what I love about this country. Freedom of speech and big stuff.

"Look at that car. Biggest car you'll ever see!"

"Yeah. But it's ugly."

"So what? Look at the size of the thing!"

"Look at the size of my penis. Goes all the way down to my ankle."

"Yeah, but you come after five seconds."

"So what? Look how big it is!"

"Look at that building. A hundred and seventy-five stories straight up into the sky!"

"Yeah, but if there was ever an accident—"

"It'd be a *huge* tragedy—bodies all over the place!"

We love big stuff. The more big stuff the better. We invented the salad bar. That was an American event. All you can eat for $2.99. Yeah. The triumph of quantity over quality. *(Crazed)* "I'll take some lettuce and olives and peppers and onions and—oh, great. They have these little red things. Some more lettuce, some cucumbers—this plate's not gonna be big enough. Honey! Get the car! Back it right up here and open the trunk! Yeah."

"Gee, pal. How much salad can you eat?"

"Shut up! What're you, Canadian or something? I paid three bucks! I can have the whole thing if I want! I'm taking *all* the salad!"

That was the original idea with the space shuttle. *(Gazing skyward)*

"Look at that space shuttle. It's something, huh?"

"What does it do?"

"Well, it goes up. And then—umm—it comes back down."

"That's it?"

"Yeah, but look how big it is! Look at the size of that cargo area. You have any idea how much salad you can fit in there?"

We've got to readjust our attitude. That's why we're in so much trouble economically. We waltzed into Japan after World War II going, "Get your asses in gear. You're gonna be democratic and capitalistic like us from now on or we'll blow you up again!"

"What do we do?"

"Well, you work hard—real hard—and eventually it will pay off. Use your head. Use your hands. Now get to work, goddamnit!"

Little did we know they would take us seriously. Now they own half of America. We were sitting around eating and farting and watching football. Meanwhile they're building advanced technology and buying real estate. *(Announcer's voice)* "America! Brought to you by—Japan! Makers of all the stuff you're too fat and lazy to make yourself!"

I love it whenever the Japan bashing heats up. Some Japanese businessman makes a comment about the laziness of American workers or some guys in Detroit get laid off because Chryslers aren't selling as well as Toyotas and that night on the news you'll see a gang of auto workers outside the plant in Michigan taking turns beating the shit out of a Hyundai with a sledgehammer. THWANG! "Take that, fuckin' Nips!" THWANG! "Yeah!" THWANG! "Cocksuckers!" THWOCK! "Kiss my American ass!" Meanwhile, in tiny little letters on the tip of the head of the hammer it says "Made in Japan."

(Thickheaded) "I just don't trust these Japs. They're fuckin' sneaky. They're Commies. Get this: they make better products that cost less and last longer. Now that's just un-American."

Iraq. Iran. Iran. Iraq. I think we should take Iraq and Iran and combine them into one country and call it Irate. All the pissed-off people live in one place and get it over with.

"Those goddamn Iratians. I hate them!"

We've got to give racists credit, though. In the face of progress and history and humanity, they've still managed to keep all the doors in their heads locked. And they've thrown away the keys.

One word, folks: racism.

"He's black, he's red, he's yellow, he's brown. I don't like him 'cause he's different from me."

Hey! My hatred is not based on color or creed. My hatred is based on performance. I have a white Irish cousin who looks exactly like me and you know what? He's an *idiot!* He's ignorant, he's lazy, he's a huge pus-filled boil on the ass of society.

"He's a wop, he's a spic, he's a mick, he's a Jew. Nigger, panface, Paddy, Limey, Nazi, raisinhead, burrboy, hooknose, greaseball, Frog, coon, Canuck, slant, jungle bunny, spear chucker . . ."

And where do you all live? New York. Right. Get in the pot, folks. Get in the great big melting pot because we're making soup. American soup.

Two words: David Duke. Two more words: nose job. I think you hear me knocking, David, and I think I'm coming in, and I'm bringing a black guy, a Jewish guy and an entire South Vietnamese family with me. And you know what we're gonna do? We're gonna burn all the sheets except one, which we're gonna turn into a giant hammock for the black guy to hang out in, and then we're gonna watch *Do the Right Thing* over and over again—until we get it right.

And guess who's making the popcorn?

(Takes deep swig of beer. Stubs out cigarette. Lights up a fresh one. Inhales. Exhales.)

We kicked Saddam's ass and now I think it's time we enjoy it. It's a stupid overblown macho feeling, but who knows when we'll be able to enjoy it again? C'mon. Buy a T-shirt. Crack open a beer. Celebrate. Let's take advantage of the situation. Let's make a couple of stops on our way home from the Gulf. First stop—Vietnam. Surprise the hell out of those people. "You make a movie?" *(Pointing gun)* "Not this time, pal. Actually, we could make a movie. We could. We've got cameras strapped to our bombs. Let's make a movie called *Watch My Village Blow Up. (Running away)* "Oh no! Francis Ford Coppola! Oliver Stone!"

Next stop. Not Russia. Not Iraq. Not Iran. Not Irate. I'll tell you where. You know where? Canada. I don't trust them! They're too nice and they're too quiet and they live right above America, okay? I think if you live in Buffalo, right at the Canadian border, and you listen very closely at night, you can hear those Canadians up there sharpening their ice skates and getting ready to come down and take our cheese! I don't trust any country with that many French-speaking people. France and the French-speaking quarter of Montreal treat Americans like shit. You know why? Because years ago they gave us the croissant. *Le qwah-soh!* What did we do? We turned it into a croissandwich. Thank you very much. You got any *pate*? Some chicken liver *pate* would be very nice! I don't pronounce it *pâté*. I'm not going to pronounce that little squiggly mark over the *e*. Okay? I'm an

American. I pay my taxes. It's *pate* as far as I'm concerned. It's like that singer *Sade.* "My named is spelled S-A-D-E but I pronounce it Shar-day." Great. My name is Denis; I'm going to pronounce it "Der-nish." Okay? We can all be French. Pronounce your name the way it's spelled. Then you can suck on my *pené,* okay? I don't have enough problems in my life worrying about cancer and tumors and war in the Persian Gulf. I have to walk into a pastry shop in the middle of Manhattan every morning going, "Yeah, give me a cup of coffee and then give me one of those . . ." What do I say? *Qwah-soh? Qwah-seh? Qwah-sah?* "Give me a fuckin' doughnut, okay, pal? Give me a doughnut with chocolate on top and nothing inside." I don't trust people who put stuff inside of doughnuts.

"Well, it's only hot blueberry sauce."

"It could be hot French semen for all I know, pal! I want a doughnut!" I've got a big French monkey on my back! Get it off me!

(Takes a long, deep swig of beer. Inhales. Exhales.)

France. A country that made Jerry Lewis famous. Jerry Lewis. For years he made millions of dollars running around like a spaz. *(Dances around stage on his ankles with arms flailing)* "Lady! Oh, lady! A-la-la-la-la-lady! Oh, Dean!" Now he spends the rest of his life trying to help kids who actually do walk that way. I thought that was nice of God. Thank you, God, for that piece of justice pie. I'll have two pieces of that pie. Okay!?

(Lights fade out)

(A single soft blue spot frames him as he sits on a crate lighting a cigarette. He inhales pensively. He exhales slowly.)

I don't know. Personally . . . I think Mama Cass said it best when she said . . . *(Suddenly choking to death)* "Achhh! ACHHH! HCHCHCH!"

(Takes a long swig of beer)

(Singing) "All the leaves are brown—all the leaves are brown—and the sky is—*(Choking)* ACHHH! ACCHHHH!"

(Inhales deeply on cigarette. Exhales with a loud choking sound.)

(Singing) "California dream—*(Choking)*—ACCH! ACCCHHH! More mustard! MORE MUSTARD! ACHHHH!"

(Inhales deeply on cigarette. Pauses. Exhales several large smoke rings. They float slowly out and above the audience.)

I'm happy the war's over, don't get me wrong. For a couple of reasons. One: peace. That's a good reason. People coming home from the Gulf? That's a great reason. The main reason I'm happy the war's over? I'll be honest with you. The yellow ribbons, okay? Because when I saw the yellow ribbons I didn't think about the hostages or the war in the Persian Gulf. I thought of one thing and one thing only: Tony Orlando and Dawn, okay? Tie a yellow ribbon around my head and shoot me. No more yellow ribbons—*ever*. I never want to see another yellow ribbon as long as I live unless it's tied around Tony Orlando's neck. Leave the old oak tree alone.

Did you ever notice they never take any fat hostages? Did you ever notice that? It's always skinny or normal-sized people, you know? It's never the big fat hellholes who could use the time in captivity. You never see a guy come out from Lebanon going, "I was held hostage for seven months and I lost 175 pounds. I feel good and I look good and I learned self-discipline. That's the important thing."

"Hi. Tommy Lasorda here. I'm held hostage during the off season and that's how I lose the weight."

George Bush made out like a bandit in that war, didn't he? He told us he was a tough guy. We didn't believe him. We knew it was just a publicity thing. But now the whole world thinks he *is* a tough guy because he won the war. He's not a tough guy. The last time we had a tough President was FDR. There was a guy in a wheelchair, with polio, and smoked three and a half packs a day in public. What a guy. "We have nothing to fear but fear itself." Yeah. And you know . . . staircases. Staircases, soccer and dancing and fear—then we're home free. And dodgeball. Staircases, soccer, dancing, fear and dodgeball. Just be afraid of those five and nothing else.

I'm pretty sure that FDR never puked in public. I'm pretty sure about that. I'm not exactly sure, but I'm pretty sure that he was never at a state dinner and went, "Well, you know, we're the most powerful . . . BLAHHH."

See, George Bush has to learn you can't be a tough guy anymore. It's not fashionable. You're not supposed to smoke or drink or eat meat or anything. Being tough is out of style.

I know there's a couple of best-selling books out on the subject of rediscovering your macho self. But those are just books boys. Just words on paper. When it comes to actions, we're not supposed to be macho anymore. Macho is just one facet of the new man. We're also supposed to be sensitive and caring and loving. We've had over twenty years with this knowledge, boys. Twenty years of the women's movement telling us what *they* want. Twenty years to develop. We have thumbs now. We're evolving. C'mon.

We're supposed to be involved in equal rights and stuff like that. We've done a lot for that, haven't we, guys? Oh yeah, we haven't done shit! But you know something, I think we should get credit for the smidgen of progress we've made as men on equal rights. Fifteen or twenty years ago we didn't care if women had orgasms. We couldn't have cared less. Now you're gonna have one if it takes us four days. We don't care how long we have to be down there. "Honey, did it happen? Well, let me get my toolbox. Hang on a second. This is a threat to my masculinity, goddamnit." Sex is supposed to be about tenderness and we've turned it into a performance sport. "Honey, did you come yet? Three times? *(Joyous, arms raised)* I'm the winner! Three to nothing! I'm the winner of the Orgasm Cup." Just so you can walk into work the next day and brag to the other guys at the office *(mouth open, frozen in a twisted position)*, "Last night was unbelievable, man. Look at my jaw. It was unbelievable." Nah, we haven't done shit for equal rights.

I thought the Anita Hill-Clarence Thomas affair was going to be the breakthrough point. National television on a weekend. Everybody's watching. I thought that come Monday morning there would be Anita Hill parades and Anita Hill buttons and Anita Hill hats. But come Monday morning the national opinion polls showed that the overwhelming majority of people in this country thought she was lying because she had something to gain. Like what? A sitcom. *(Television announcer's voice)* " 'The Anita Hill Show!' The kooky adventures of that crazy sexual harassment gal! This week she finds a pubic hair in her Coke! The kooky adventures of Anita Hill. Tuesdays at nine!"

I believe in equal rights right down the line. Equal rights, equal jobs, equal pay. I think we have to be politically correct on this issue. But I'm gonna be honest with you. I don't care how far we drive down the Equal Rights Turnpike. I don't care how politically correct we get—I still love breasts. I love them. And if you think that's politically incorrect, I have some news for you. Even lesbians love them. As a matter of fact, I think they do a better job than men because to them breasts are just a part of the whole of their loved one. That's too easy for men, isn't it? No. We can't just love you. We have to worship your breasts.

(Crazed) "The breasts we have just are not satisfactory. They're too small. We have to build new ones."

I don't understand the fascination with breast implants. I like the real thing no matter what the size. I like big ones. I like small ones. I think I even like the smaller ones better than the big ones. I love all shapes, all sizes. I love the ones that are shaped like golf balls, I love the ones that are shaped like teardrops. I like the melons and the pears, the footballs and the ferns. I love the ones shaped like LBJ's head. I love them all—as long as they're real.

The fascination with perfect breasts has gone too far. Look, all of us think we are imperfect. Everyone. I'm sure even Cindy Crawford wakes up in the morning, looks in the mirror and says, "You know what I need? A third breast, right in between the two other ones."

But the advances in cosmetic surgery have taken a turn for the worse. People who can afford it are having stuff done every day. And they're all having stuff removed. Michael Jackson has his nose taken off, Liz Taylor has her thighs shaved down, people are having their love handles sucked out and made into paperweights. If I had the money I wouldn't have stuff removed. I'd have stuff added on. I'd have penises all over my body. In my armpits, behind my knees, on my arms. I'd have seven penises. I'd be Penis Man. I'd walk into the men's room and go, "Get outta my way, boys. *(Turning around in a circle)* I gotta take a piss!"

Men haven't really caught up with the cosmetic surgery revolution yet. It's mostly women. But the future is now, boys. Let me tell you a little story. I was reading the newspaper one morning about seven months ago. If you're like me, you read the front page first—just to see what the disease update is—any new cures or causes—find out if we're going to blow up tomorrow—and then skip right to the sports section. Now as I flip to the sports section I usually flip a page at a time, looking for ads for free VCRs and little stories about really funny deaths. So this one morning I'm on page 16 of the *New York Times* and something catches my eye—the corner of my eye—and I glance down and a headline grabs my attention: "Man's Penis Cut Off in Industrial Accident." Page 16. Now every guy in the world is thinking the same thing I am. "Page 16?" If this was the *Guy Gazette*, that story would be on page 1. There'd be a big picture of the guy. *(Frozen scared expression)* "AHHHH!"

Now I start to read the article. It's tiny. A few paragraphs. First paragraph says: (AP) Some town in upstate New York. "A worker at a manufacturing plant in this town had his penis severed while working on the assembly line yesterday." Now, let's stop right there. Guys, let me ask you something. Do you recall in your travels through life—from childhood through grade school into

101

high school and college and beyond—do you recall any-one—your dad, a high school guidance counselor, your best friend, a cop—ever telling you about a job in which your penis had to be hanging out? I mean, besides por-nography? No. No such job exists. That leaves us with two options. Number one: he was jerking off. Very un-likely. Number two: he was doing what a lot of guys like to do when they are kidding around—it's a male bonding thing. He pulled out his penis and went, "Hey, guys! Look at this! Hah-hah! Look at my—BANG! It's gone!" What a moment that must have been. One moment he's got his manhood in his hand and the next moment—BANG!—it's zipping down the assembly line. Wow. One second he's Superman, the next second he's Captain Eu-nuch.

Okay. The second paragraph begins: "A new penis was built and successfully attached after seven hours of sur-gery at Rochester General." Wait a minute. Hang on. A new penis was built? Out of what? Old penises? Are they cutting the penises off of dead guys and saving them? Are they using meat? Are they using Play-doh? A new penis was built. Now, we all know how advanced emer-gency medical services are. We've all heard stories about people having a foot or an arm or a finger chopped off; they rush the person and the severed appendage on ice to the hospital—seven coworkers standing around going: "I ain't picking it up. No way." Even the EMTs, when they got there, took one look at the floor and went: "For-get it. We'll build you a new one. Let's go."

A new penis was built. That's why the story was on page 16. They don't want men to find out about this. Think of that poor guy. His penis is cut off. They rush him to the hospital. They've stopped the bleeding. He's sitting in a trauma room, staring at his crotch. "God. I might as well just get some breasts and a vagina now."

The doctor walks in. "Well, son. We've got good news and bad news. The bad news is—your penis has been cut off. The good news is—we're gonna build you a new one. I just need to know one thing. How big was your old penis?" "Oh . . . ohhhh . . . well, Doc, it was huge. Musta been seventeen inches. That's why they couldn't pick it up off the floor." That's why the story was on page 16. They don't want men to find out about this. There'd be lines of men outside every hospital with a knife in one hand and their penis in the other. "Yeah. Need to see a doctor. My penis has been cut off. It was about twenty inches long."

Men haven't really discovered the implant route. Not when it comes to the penis. We're still too busy worrying about our hair. What is it with bald men? Why can't they just be bald? I hate these guys who go bald and then take their life savings and get one of those weave jobs, or the really bad toupee that kind of looks real from the front but has those telltale signs at the side. And they just show up one day with a full head of hair and they think we don't notice. You know what I'm going to do when I go bald? You know what I'm going to wear on my head? A cat. A fluffy blond cat. Just walk into work one day— *(Taken aback)* "Denis . . . you look so much . . . younger." *(Whispering)* "I've got a cat on my head. Don't tell anyone."

As enlightened as men think they are, they still don't know what makes women work. Every year polls ask women what they find attractive about men, and the most popular answer is always the same—a sense of humor. Not penis size, not cash, not car—a sense of humor. Yeah, right. Didn't work for the elephant man, now did it? He could have cultivated the greatest sense of humor in the history of civilization. He could be spewing witticism after witticism, telling bawdy jokes, doing impressions. *(As elephant man)* "Uhhng. Unggh." At the end of the night, he still isn't getting laid. He's hearing the same old explanations. "Well, I think you're really funny. When you sucked that whole jar of peanuts through your nose I was on the floor in hysterics. And I think you're really attractive, except for like . . . your head . . . and that big squiggly thing sticking out of your neck."

(Stubs out cigarette in ashtray. Takes a swig of beer.)

There are two sets of rules in this country. There's one for men and one for women, that's the way it works, you know? It's never better exemplified than in Hollywood, where the rules are written by men and for men. Where every actress, when she first starts out, in her first couple of movies, has to show her breasts. Isn't that the unwritten rule? Doesn't matter who it is. Ellen Barkin, Jane Fonda, Daryl Hannah—politically active or not— every actress, for the first couple of movies, is forced to show her breasts and then—*(Authoritative)* "You're free to go." But men don't have to show their penises. It's totally unfair. I don't want to hear about Mel Gibson's ass and Kevin Costner's ass—we all have asses. It's not the same thing. Men should be forced to show their penises in the movies, okay? I don't care how bluntly it's done. I don't care if Robert De Niro, in the first scene of his first movie, just walks up to the camera and says, "Here's my penis. Now let's get on with the plot. Whaddya say?" Maybe we line up the whole cast right at the beginning of the movie. "Here are the breasts, here's the penis. Let's get on with the story." I'll be honest with you. I'm heterosexual and even I want to see Kevin Costner's penis, okay? Just for a second. Is there a spot on it or a wolf tattoo? I don't know. *Dances With My Penis*, starring Kevin Costner. You know that would be a big rental video. "Honey, rewind that. That is a buffalo. I'm sorry, I thought it was a wolf but it's a buffalo."

We're supposed to be able to cry now, guys. You know that. It's difficult because, you know, we're brought up as men with that genetic sort of macho thing in our DNA. Then, you know, growing up, we're taught to be men. "Be a man! Keep it inside. Be a man. Hey. Ho. Huh." So you have to kind of retrain yourself. It's difficult. I'll give you an example: I went to see the movie *E.T.* when it first came out. This is ten years ago, so I was a much younger guy. I went to see it the first week it opened. I went to see it with two friends of mine—two guys I grew up with, sort of Boston street-tough Irish guys. Mike McGinn and Noose O'Neal (whose real name was Ed but we called him Noose because his dad tried to commit suicide in the basement one time by throwing a rope over a rafter and standing on a chair, but the chair slipped and the rafter broke and he ended up splitting his head open, and now his kid's called Noose for the rest of his life. And his poor dad was bald, so he had to walk around with a scar on his head for the rest of *his* life). So the three of us go to the movies. Now if you remember, in retrospect, *E.T.* might seem like it was a stupid movie. But didn't you get sucked in the first time you saw it? It was really kind of manipulative. I'm watching the movie and all of a sudden I get sucked in. The little puppet's phoning home and the kid crying and all of a sudden I go soft. *(About to cry)* "Mmmphf!" Tears are welling up in my eyes. I'm straining to hold them back. "Mmmphf . . . mmp." Now the kid's waving good-bye to E.T. and I'm about to burst. "Mmmmp-mmmphf-mmphf!" I want to cry but I'm afraid to cry because I don't want my friends to think I'm quote/unquote "faggy." So I'm sitting there going, "Mmmmmmphf," and I glance over at Mike and Noose and they're both going, "Mmmmphf," because they don't

want me to think that they're quote/unquote "faggy."
Meanwhile, we're sitting in the "I am not a homosexual"
seating arrangement that heterosexual men use when
they go to the movies. You know what I'm talking about?
It was me, an empty seat, Mike McGinn, an empty seat,
and Noose O'Neal. How insecure about your sexuality
could you possibly be?

"I think Denis is a homo."

"Why?"

"He sat right next to me at the movie theatre last
night and he cried when E.T. phoned home. He's a girl.
He probably wears a bra. He's a fagboy. He's a mo-man.
He's a queerbait. Denis Queery, that's his name!"

All that testosterone we use coming up with names for
each other—"fagboy," "fagman." You can still go to the
movie today and see two guys with a seat in between
them. Grown men. Sitting in the "I am not a homo" arrangement. One guy whispering out of the side of his
mouth, "Don't sit in that fucking seat. Just put your coat
there. Jesus. Whatsa matter with you? Don't touch me
with your elbow or anything, okay? And you better not
cry at the sad part."

I'll give you a better example, a more recent example.
I think it gets more difficult to deal with the older you
get. I have a son who's eighteen months old now. He was
born three months premature—dangerously premature.
He was two pounds when he was born. He was in intensive care for three months. He was about the size of my
hand. Tiny. Minuscule. Now, I am not a religious guy, but
everyday I would go to the hospital and sit next to the
machine he was in—this techno-bed with plastic see-
through sides—and pray: "Please, God. Let him get better. Please let him get better. Please please please
please."

He slowly gets better. . . . We bring him home. He's

106

home for about a month. We take him back for his big checkup. The doctor looks him over. He says, "He's A-OK. He's gonna be fine!" And as soon as I heard those words, the macho button snapped back on in my head and I was transformed. *(Chest puffed out)* "Of course he's gonna be fine. Of course it only took six months instead of nine because . . . because . . . because . . . my semen is so strong, that's why! My wife gets pregnant on Tuesday, we have a baby on Thursday, for crissakes. I masturbate and there's a kid there in the morning! Who do you think you're talking to? You're talking to Penis Man!"

I know I get it from my father. I think most men get their behavior patterns from their fathers. My dad was a great guy: an Irish immigrant, a real World War II-John Wayne-Ted Williams kind of guy. He had a big chest full of rippling muscles. He was an auto mechanic for thirty-five years—an ultra-macho job—fixing engines, covered in grease, smelling like gas.

He had a basement full of tools. He could do any job: carpentry, electronics. He was always fixing things around the house. We started out with a two-room apartment and we ended up with eighteen rooms—straight up into the sky. Paneling in every room. What is it about Irish immigrants and paneling? Does anybody know? It's like you get off the boat at Ellis Island and forget about that Freedom of Speech, we just want some paneling. That's all we want! He had paneling on the ceiling, on the floor. My mother had a dress made out of paneling. "Get the Murphy's Oil Soap, boys. I'm going dancing tonight."

On my brother's tenth birthday—I was six—we had a little birthday party. Just me, my brother, and my mom. And a chocolate cake. And little birthday hats. Singing the birthday song. "Happy birthday to you! Happy birthday to you!"

My dad was putting paneling in the living room during the ten minutes we weren't in there. He was working with a circular saw. So this was the sound effect we heard come echoing down the hallway during the birthday song: "Happy birthday to you. Happy birth—" *(Loud buzzing sound)* "Zzzazow zzzazow zzzzzazazazow zzzzzazazow THA-THINK!"

And my dad comes waltzing gingerly into the kitchen with his thumb hanging off at the bone. We're sitting there in our paper hats with chocolate cake in front of us —our faces frozen in fear. I'm thinking, "Wow. Dad's thumb is hanging off. Look at all that blood. Look at the bones. He's probably gonna start crying any second now."

And this is what my father says—his thumb is literally hanging by a thread of a bone, there's blood everywhere, and he says—and I quote *(calmly)*, "We got any tape around here? I need to tape this baby up." My mother snapped. She starts screaming, "I'll drive you to the hospital! Call the hospital! Tell them we're coming! Ahhhh!" But he wouldn't let my mother drive him to the hospital. That was too much of a threat to his masculinity—to be seen in a car driven by a woman. So he taped up his thumb with black electrical tape and drove himself—minus one thumb—to the hospital. Never blinked an eye. He was humming as he taped it up in front of us.

We're sitting at the table—paper hats, chocolate cake, blood, bits of bone. I looked at my brother and said, "Hey, pal. Forget about crying. Crying is over. We're never going to be able to cry about anything ever, okay? Our authority figure is a man who could sever his own head with a chainsaw, and he'd staple-gun it back on. *(Holding head on neck with one hand and a staple gun in the other)* "Fuckin' head came off." *(Stapling)* PUN-

CHIT! PUN-CHIT PUN-CHIT PUN-CHIT! Scarred us for life.

(Swigs beer. Lights up cigarette. Inhales. Exhales.)

Two years later my brother shoots an arrow into my head.

(Inhales. Exhales.)

I'll explain how this happened.

(Takes a long swig of beer)

My brother's best friend was this kid Cliffy DeCorsey, who lived up the block from us. So this one Christmas Cliffy DeCorsey's family give him a bow and arrow set as a Christmas present. Not like a fake, TV, plastic, kid's bow and arrow set. No, a real hunting bow and arrow set! Parents were nuts in the sixties. We got weapons for Christmas every year. We got hunting knives and BB guns and the Rifleman rifle that used to shoot plastic bullets—the same bullets they use now in Northern Ireland. Parents were nuts back in the sixties! "Here ya go, son. Here's a bomb. Take it out and play with it. Go ahead. Take some meat with ya, it's Christmas. Get out there and play."

So I'm in the alley—in between the building I grew up in and the building next door—it's about five feet wide— I'm just hanging out. And my brother and Cliffy appear down at the end of the alley. With the bow and arrow set. With the sun gleaming off of the bow and arrow set. My brother was an authority figure to me, as well. He was four years older than me. He was twice my size. He was worldly. He was twelve. I was only eight. I always listened to whatever it was he had to say. And what he had to say this time was: "Hey, Denis, go down and stand at the end of the alley in front of the garage door. We're gonna play William Tell, all right?" I didn't know who William Tell was. I was just so happy that the older guys were playing with me and I got in front of the garage door and was like, "Okay. Who's William Tell? Is it me? Is it you? Is it Cliffy?" Then my brother takes the luckiest shot anyone has ever taken with a bow and arrow the first time they shot in their lives. He pulled that baby back—"Unnngh!"—and let the arrow fly—"Tsssssssssss" —and the arrow landed right in my head—"Tssssss-TWONNNGGGG." Right in my head. Right above the eyes. Right here, at my widow's peak. They both made the same face. The same face at the same time. They both went *(scared stiff)*, "AHHHH!"—and ran away. Remember when you were a kid, whenever you got into trouble you could just run away? That was your first instinct. *(Running)*

"Run away!"

"Where?"

"Anywhere! Spain! Russia! China! Run away!!"

Now I make the long march upstairs with the arrow in my head. I'm not crying. I'm afraid to cry. I walk up two flights of stairs. Clomp, clomp. Clomp, clomp. Into the kitchen. Clomp, clomp. Where my parents are drinking Lipton tea and eating scones. I go, "Dad, Johnny shot an arrow into my head!" My father doesn't even blink about this, like it's the most normal thing in the world—like there's roving gangs of Indians all over the city. He just goes, "C'mere. . . . C'mere! . . . C'MERE!" Here comes the worst part. You know what's coming next, don't you? Oh yes. *(Pulling arrow from head)* THWOP! Owww. Remember that? Remember how much it hurt when they pulled the arrow from your head? Remember? No! You don't remember! NONE OF YOU REMEMBER! I'm the only guy who knows! It was General Custer and then me. My father looks down at the gaping hole in my head and goes, "Just put a piece of tape or some Band-aids on that." My mother goes, "You drive him to the hospital, mister. He just had an arrow shot into his head, for Christ's sake."

Cut to the car. I'm on the passenger side, still not crying, a big hole in my head, blood trickling between my eyes. And my dad's driving the car. Driving the car pissed off. Driving the car under duress to the hospital. Pissed off because this is more time taken out of his paneling mission. There was actually paneling on the sides of the car—it was one of those station wagons with wood trim. And he glances over at me. *(Annoyed)* "It doesn't hurt, does it?" Hurt? HURT? No, Dad, it feels great! Why don't you shoot a few more arrows into my head? Why don't you just stab me a few times, for Christ's sake? I'm eight, can I cry, please? I should be able to cry and get free stuff for a year. I'm sure if there was a Kid Injury Equivalent Chart, next to "Arrow in the Head" it would say "Free stuff and crying for a year." I get to the hospital and get ten stitches in my head and a free lollipop. "Oh, thank you. That'll fit right in the fuckin' hole. Thank you." A free lollipop? I don't want a lollipop. Get me money. That's what kids should get when they go to the hospital. Not ice cream, or candy, or comic books. Money. Cold hard cash. "Let me see—you get three million dollars."

But the story has a happy ending. When we got home my brother got the shit beat out of him by my father. That was one of the great beatings of the sixties, man. Forget about Jerry Quarry versus Muhammad Ali. My father versus my brother. TKO first round. There was a great moment in that round when my brother was on the floor in the hallway and my father was standing above him with a clenched fist going, "How'd you like an arrow shot into your head?" I was like, "Yeah, let's put him in front of the garage door and fill him full of lollipop holes, c'mon." My brother tried to assassinate me about five times in between the first Kennedy assassination and the second one.

My dad was a great guy. He just did not know pain. He just did not recognize it.

About two years after the arrow incident, we were sitting in the living room watching "Superman" on TV. The show is over. The credits are rolling. And my brother turns to me. He says, "You know, if you get a cape—you can fly just like Superman." I was shocked. "Really? All you need is the cape? Wow. But we don't have any capes, Johnny." This is where older brothers had it over younger brothers. Older brothers had the secret rule book with the special rules explained in detail. "It doesn't have to be an actual cape. It could be anything shaped like a cape. Go upstairs and get a towel!"

I ran upstairs, grabbed a blue bath towel, rushed back down, and my brother safety-pins it to my shirt. He goes into the kitchen and gets some bacon grease out of the refrigerator. Now, my parents were in the kitchen having coffee—they see my brother come into the kitchen, grab a cannister full of bacon grease and leave—don't you think that should have aroused some suspicion? Wouldn't a fourteen-year-old normally be looking for a Coke or a sandwich or some cookies?

"Where are you going with that bacon grease, son?"

"I'm gonna put it in Denis's hair to make him look like Superman and then he's gonna jump out the window and crash to his death."

"Oh. Okay. Don't get any blood on the paneling."

He puts the bacon grease in my hair and I must admit —it was a stroke of genius. I looked great. Just like Superman. Then he lays out my flight pattern. "See that chair over there? All you gotta do is jump off it, stick your arms straight out like Superman, and you'll fly across the room. I'll be waiting for you over here on the couch."

Now, in between the chair and the couch was this huge wooden coffee table. It was the size of a coffin—I think my old Irish uncles were buried in there—Uncle Fitzy or Uncle Sully or somebody. They couldn't afford to bury them so they kept them in the living room. And it had these jagged Nazi edges on it. So I get up on the chair, I stick out my arms and I announce myself: "Here I come, Johnny! Faster than a speeding bullet! Here I come!" And I jump off. And I fly! I actually flew! I flew a good three or four feet. Straight across the room. I remember the thrill of being airborne. I remember the ecstasy of the air. I remember looking down and thinking, "Uh-oh." SCRUNCH! Right onto the edge of the coffee table. "Oww! Oww!" My face embedded on the corner of the coffin. "Owww! Oww!" William Holden. "Owwwww!"

My brother got the shit beat out of him for that one, too. *(Angry Dad voice)* "HOW'D YOU LIKE A COFFEE TABLE IMBEDDED IN YOUR HEAD?" My brother had a lot of shots of my father from the floor up back in the sixties. *(Looking up)* "Gee, Dad. You got a lotta hair sticking outta your nose."

About 1978—I'd been out of the house for four years at that point—I went back to visit my father and he's putting up new paneling over the old paneling. "You've gotta keep up to date, son," he said. He's got one of those pump-action nail guns—they fire the nail like a bullet into the wall. He was talking to me and he lost his place and BAM! he fired one right into the middle of his palm. Like Jesus. And then he pulls it out with his teeth. I was like, "Holy shit." I never saw his balls but they must have been huge, folks. "Son, give me a hand with these balls—I can't get them into my pants. Jesus. They're huge." He was unbelievable. He smoked five packs of cigarettes a day. Didn't even have his own brand. He would go into a store and come out with five different brands—Marlboros, Kools, Kents, Camels. As if he were a wine taster. *(Inhaling, dwelling on the smoke)* "A very fresh bouquet." *(Exhaling)* "A fine after-dinner smoke. Great with meat."

(Stubs out cigarette. Takes a long, deep swig of beer. Pauses.)

He would smoke cigars, Tiparillos, pipes—anything. He ate meat for breakfast, lunch and dinner. Steak and eggs, steak and soup, steak and potatoes, steak and steak. A hard, hard man. Then in 1985, to celebrate his sixtieth birthday, he goes back to Ireland to visit the village he grew up in and see his brothers and his sisters and his cousins. My father came from a family with seven thousand kids. One of those huge Irish families. You can take a walking tour of Ireland and every five feet you will run into a guy who looks like my dad.

"Are you by any chance related to—"

"I'm his second cousin."

Two days after his sixtieth birthday, he's in a pub in Killarney, County Kerry. It's the southwestern part of Ireland—the most beautiful part. His hometown. He's with several of his brothers and sisters. He lights up a cigarette, smiles and BANG! He was dead before he hit the floor.

(Pauses. Takes a deep breath. Lights up a cigarette. Inhales. Exhales.)

Gone.
Over.
Passed on.
No longer with us.
Ceased to be.

(Inhales deeply. Pauses. Exhales.)

That'll pop your little macho balloon. When the guy you think is always going to be there—the John Wayne, Ted Williams guy—is dead. In a millisecond. In a sliver of time so small it cannot even be measured. How long does it take to fall from a standing position onto the floor? And where in that little window of time do you actually leave this earth?

In the coffin at the wake you could see—through all that funeral makeup—this bruise on his forehead. Where he landed. The doctor in Ireland had assured my mother, "He never felt that."

I remember touching his hands when he was in the coffin. They were folded across his chest. They were cold. Not like ice. Like marble.

I got a phone call from somebody. From my Uncle Patrick. He made the call because he wanted to soften the blow. He was with my father. He was standing next to him, held my father's head in his arms while they were waiting for the ambulance. My father's mother had died giving birth to the last child and my Uncle Patrick—the oldest—had raised the kids while my grandfather worked the farm. Here he was—stuck in this twisted mother and child mosaic—trying to make me feel better. He said, "We were having a couple of drinks and I was telling him a joke—about the monk and the mule—and I told him the punch line and he laughed and then he went down."

He died with a smile on his face. You try to grab on to that. "Yeah, that makes me feel better. He was smiling. That's good. It makes it easier." But it doesn't really. The only good thing about going that way is this: it's a gift. There's no pain, no struggle, no light, no tunnel. One second you are an Irish immigrant. The next second you are face to face with God. *(Shaking God's hand)* "How ya doin', God? Got any cigarettes up here? I think you could use some paneling up there behind Elvis. Just a suggestion."

My brother and my sister Ann and I were here. My mother and my sister Betsy were overseas with my dad. That was a hell of a flight for my mother. Coming home empty-handed. On the phone she said, "You don't know what it's like to lose your best friend." I'd never thought of it that way. She was my ma. He was my dad. I had never seen it from their side. They'd known each other since they were children. They grew up in the same village. I can't imagine how empty she must feel. How alone, sometimes.

We had to wait for a week after my mother came back before the body was flown over. My Uncle Patrick wanted to have a wake and funeral in Killarney. We sat around the kitchen table with my overweight Irish aunts and my weathered, leather-necked Irish uncles and traded stories about my dad. We ate bad Irish food. Boiled beef. Boiled meatballs. Boiled cabbage. Boiled to the point where it actually has no advantage as a piece of roughage. Do you know how long you have to boil cabbage before it gets that soft? Ten years. My aunts actually boil cabbage around the clock and jar it ten years before it's scheduled to be eaten.

My Aunt Margaret said that we should thank God he died in Ireland. Now everyone who knew him would get the chance to say good-bye. All of the Irish. All of the Irish who had moved to America. We had to add an extra day to the wake here. There were lines a full block long for four hours at a time. People we never knew coming to pay their respects. An old woman who said my father had fixed her car without charging her for the last few years because her husband passed away and she had no money. A woman my age who said her car broke down in a blizzard and no one would stop and after two hours my dad pulled over, fixed her car and followed her home to make sure she got there safely.

As we left the church to drive to the cemetery, this guy who sold newspapers at the end of our block growing up—this bent old ink-stained little man—stood on the sidewalk and saluted the coffin. With tears in his eyes. He said my father had always been so nice to him. My Aunt Margaret said it reminded her of President Kennedy.

The last time I saw my father was at Logan Airport in Boston. I drove him and my mother and Betsy to the airport that day. Followed them right up to the metal detector. As my dad went through the beeper went off. They made him empty his pockets. He pulled out a pack of Marlboros, a pack of Newports and a small silver chain —his St. Christopher medal. That was the last shot I had of him. Shaking his head and laughing. St. Christopher set off the security alarm.

I didn't cry. I held it in. We grew up without home movies. We couldn't afford them. We got a slide projector in 1968. We thought that catapulted us right into the middle class. A slide projector? Wow. *(Pressing the slide-changer button)* PUN-CHIT PUN-CHIT PUN-CHIT. We watched all those slides the night after we got the news. But to this day I have never watched the video-tapes I made of my father in the eighties because I know if I see him walking and talking—there's going to be crying like you've never seen before. There's going to be a crying festival at my apartment. People flying in from other countries.

"Have you seen Denis lately?"

"No. Apparently he's holed up in his house watching videos and putting up paneling."

No. I did the macho thing. I sucked it up. I got that lump in my throat. "Mmmmphf!" People must have thought I was a nut at the wake and the funeral.

"Sorry for your troubles, Denis."

"Mmmmphf."

I did the Irish macho thing. Held it all in. Friends were telling me, "You should talk to somebody. A therapist or psychologist."

"Mmmmphf. I'm not talking to anybody. I'm going to hold it all in until my blood pressure rises and I have an aneurism and my head blows up."

I couldn't picture myself in an analyst's office. "How do you feel about your father's death?" *(About to blow up)* "Mmmmmmmmmpfh . . . mmmmmmpfh . . . MMM—" *(Head blows up)* KER-SPLOIT!

I would see things that reminded me of my father—a John Wayne movie or a Red Sox game—and it would plant that knot in my neck—"Mmmmmmphf!" For years I walked around with that rock inside of me. For six years it was bubbling right below the surface.

It wasn't until I got married and had a child that things began to change. All of a sudden I was in therapy. I was in this perverted Irish macho therapy. This twisted plateau of healing.

(Working it out) "Oh no, no, thank you. I don't need any help now. I'm fine. I'm doing it myself. I'm taking all

that Dad stuff from my father and filtering it down through me and into my son. I'm fine. I'm feeling fine."

I know that's a cliché, that you change when you've got a kid. I also know it's the big fashion thing right now. Back in the eighties it was cocaine. Now it's "Here's my kid. He matches my couch."

But it's true. Soon—very soon—after you have a kid there's an immediate slap in the face. Reality cologne. Life is no longer about luxury. It's not stereos and CD players and Jeep Cherokees. It's the basics. Food and shelter. Hot and cold. Sleep. Feces. Urine. Blood. Then there's a wave that washes over you. You find yourself in a dimly lit room, late at night, staring down into the crib. Whispering. "Look at this. Look at this creature. Look at this sinless, cold-sober, empty little vessel . . . waiting to be filled up with ingredients . . . and it's up to me and my wife. We can fill him up with anything. Love. Or hate. Or indifference."

Then it's just a short hop, skip and a jump to the other line of thinking: "Oh. Now I see. Now I know why I have a responsibility to the planet. Because I want my son to have a better life."

I'm not a guy who gets involved. I deal in angst. I deal in cynicism. I vote. But I vote pessimistically. I reserve the right to keep my distance. To judge. To point my finger and parade.

Now I realize if I want to change the world, if it can be changed, I've got to get involved. I've got to get my hands on civil rights and all these things I supposedly believe in. I've got to get in position on the power role. Get active. March. Maraud. Get some heart behind my head. So that maybe—twenty-five years from now—my son can live in a city without race problems. In a country without color. In a world without war. So that maybe— twenty-five years from now—he can turn to me one day, put his hand on my shoulder and say, "You know something, Dad? I really like this place." And I can honestly answer: "Well, son. I did my best."

And other times, I think: "Hey, fuck him."

I didn't break the planet, okay? It was like this when I found it. I'm sick and tired of my generation getting blamed for the condition of the planet. I'm sick and tired of my generation being called "The TV Generation."

(Whining) "Well, all you guys did was watch TV."

What did you expect? We watched Lee Harvey Oswald get shot to death live on TV one Sunday morning when we were six years old. We were afraid to change the channel for the next thirty years.

"Hey. This show sucks."

"Yeah, but somebody might get shot during the commercial. Hang on."

Bang bang bang bang.

(The small blue spot fades to black)

DEATH

(The lights blast up full as he puts the match to another cigarette. He is now standing center stage.)

That's the problem with this country. We always shoot all the wrong guys. We shoot JFK, we shoot RFK and it comes to Teddy, we go, "Ah, leave him alone. He'll screw it up himself, no problem, you know?" He's the biggest target in the whole goddamn Kennedy family—and nobody takes a shot at him. He weighs about 7000 pounds. You could shoot a bullet in Los Angeles and hit him in the ass in Boston five minutes later. He'd be standing on the lawn at the Kennedy compound going, "Uh, there's a . . . uh . . . bullet . . . uh, uh . . . in, uh . . . my, uh . . . uh, uhh . . . ass, uh."

Ted Kennedy. Good senator but a bad date. You know what I'm saying? One of those guys who gets home around midnight and says, "What did I forget? Oh! The girl! Damnit! I've gotta start remembering these things." You know what I'm saying? I think you do. I think you hear me knocking and I think I'm coming in. And guess what? All I'm wearing is a shirt.

Ted Kennedy sitting on the Sexual Harassment Committee. Cut me a giant piece of big-break pie. Ted Kennedy sitting up on the dais—all 7000 pounds of him—going, "I'm finally an expert and I can't even open my mouth. Wow."

See, I grew up in Massachusetts as a working-class Irish kid. We adored the Kennedys.

We had this love/hate relationship with them. We loved to elect them, but we hated them because they had so much money. We loved to see them get into trouble, but we hated them because they always got away with it.

But I had to draw the line long before the Easter Rape Weekend. I had to draw a giant line. I had to draw the line at the Rose Kennedy birthday party a couple of summers ago. Now, if you're a hundred—have a party. But do it in private because you probably don't look too good. Not the Kennedys. No. Since it was Mrs. Kennedy it was on the cover of *People* magazine and on CNN. They wheeled her out onto the lawn at Hyannisport—there must have been two thousand Kennedys out there. She has no idea where she is. The wheelchair's rolling. She's in a trance. *(Waving erratically)* "Where's Jack? Where's Bobby?" She's lucky Teddy wasn't pushing the chair. "No. Teddy. Not off of the bridge. . . . Noooooooo—" SPLASH.

There's another cliché about the Kennedys. That the world was a bright and shining place until JFK was snatched away. But there's an element of truth to that. That's why it's become a cliché. After JFK died, the war in Vietnam escalated. Then Bobby died and the war got worse. Then we had drugs. Then we had bell-bottoms. Then Casey Kasem had his own TV show. Then we had more drugs and more bell-bottoms and more drugs and guns and crime and poverty and more guns and more crime.

We have a real problem with crime in this country. And we have a real problem with guns. Just exactly what is going on down at the post office? Every other year some postal worker snaps and takes out twelve of his ex-coworkers in a hail of gunfire. If I was a supervisor down at the post office, I wouldn't lay anybody off for the next ten years.

"Hanrahan! Whaddaya doing?"

"Nothing."

"Well, um, uhh . . . keep it up. You're doing a great job!"

We've got some heavy metal nuts crawling out of cages in this country. Jeffrey Dahmers. Hey. I'm a meat eater, but that's taking it a little bit too far. He was taking human meat sandwiches to work, for crissake. You know there had to be one of his ex-coworkers watching the report on CNN and going, "Uh-oh. Oh, my God. I traded my tuna fish sandwich with him one day! *(Spitting)* Ugh. Acch! Acchh!"

Jeffrey. *(Shaking head)* Jeffrey, Jeffrey, Jeffrey.

He would kill men. Then fuck them. Then eat them. You see, Jeffrey was no different from the rest of us. We've all been at wakes. We've all gazed into the casket. We've all said aloud, "He looks so good." Jeffrey just took it one step further. "He looks *real* good."

The problem with guys like Jeffrey who push the envelope this far is that they make people who just *kill* look good.

"You killed four people?"

"Yes, your honor, I did."

"You didn't eat any of 'em, did ya?"

"No, sir."

"Oh, well, then. You're free to go. I don't want any sickos going free, but you're different. You showed some restraint."

It's usually someone you know who will kill you. Stats show that most murders are committed by loved ones against loved ones. Most shootings happen in the home. You are safe on the streets. It's once you enter the house that you have to be careful. "Honey, I'm home!" BLAM BLAM BLAM BLAM! Homeless people live forever. It's the people with the houses who are dying young. "Why are you walking the streets?" "I wanna live!"

Guns are so plentiful in this country. Every week there's a nut on a roof with a rifle and a grudge to settle. I used to get worried whenever Gorbachev visited America. He's got the bullseye right on his head. It would be easy to get off in court. "I'm sorry, your honor, but I thought it was a sign from God."

(Stubs out cigarette in ashtray. Takes a long deep swig of beer. Lights up. Inhales. Exhales with a loud spitting sound.)

And I am sick and tired of New York taking the blame for the crime problem in this country. Whenever you see a fact chart it always says that Detroit and Washington lead the world in crime and murder but New York takes the blame. "New York is a cesspool. It's a cesspool of crime and filth. We're leaving." Hey, I moved here four years ago just when it got bad. You know why? This is the most exciting place in the world to live. There are so many ways to die in New York City, c'mon! Subway crashes, drive-by shootings, race riots, construction cranes collapsing on the sidewalks, manhole covers blowing up and asbestos shooting into the sky. Every time you leave your house in this city could be the last time you ever see your loved ones alive. "Cover me, I'm going out for cigarettes!" We had a subway crash here a few months ago. The next day they found out the driver was drunk and hooked on crack. Folks, this makes Disneyland look like a bike ride, doesn't it? "Your driver today is Edward, he's drunk and hooked on crack, the train has no brakes and the man sitting next to you has a loaded 9mm. Good luck, folks."

(Hanging from strap) "Honey! Get the camera out! This is gonna be great!" People who live in New York wear that fact like a badge on our sleeves. We're proud of living here because we know it impresses *everybody*.

"I was in Vietnam."

"So what? I live in New York."

"Really? Wow. How do you do it?"

Every place else on the East Coast has four seasons, we have five. Winter, spring, summer, HELL and fall. HELL. You know those three weeks right at the end of the summer? When it's 175 degrees out? When the streets begin to melt. When people just snap every minute of the day. People just shoot each other indiscriminately. Even the cops can't take it. "Did you shoot that guy? Awright. Don't worry, we're not going to arrest you. It's too hot. Just go home."

That three-week period is just going to get worse as time goes on and the hole in the ozone gets bigger. Eventually it will be 150 degrees and snowing all summer long.

"Jesus. It's snowing."

"I know. I'm sweatin' my ass off."

That's what I love about New York. It teaches you to live life the way it should be lived—moment to moment. Because every moment in New York could be your last.

Every half moment could be your last half moment. *(Pointing to man in front row)* You! You could be walking to work tomorrow morning. Feeling good about yourself. Drink-free. Drug-free. Then somebody accidentally nudges their poodle off of a seventy-fifth-floor ledge. TOINK. *(Watches poodle fall)* "Barwwwwwwwwww."

He's headed for the ground at 175,000 miles per hour. KER-CHUNK! He's imbedded in your head. You are dead on contact. The headline in the *Post* the next day reads "Man Killed by Best Friend." People chop the article out and hang it up at the office. They laugh over it. They think it's just the funniest thing. And you are forever remembered as the Poodle Man.

"I knew the Poodle Man and, ironically, he hated dogs."

(Inhales deeply. Exhales while barking.)

New York teaches you to live life moment to moment and beat to beat. And street to street.

(The low, moody murmur of spasmodic guitar chords begins to play in the background)

We've all played that game New York: good block, bad block. *(Circling the stage)* "Good block, bad block . . . gun block, crack block . . . asbestos block . . . *(Covering head)* Poodle block! Poodle block!"

It's not just New York anymore. It could be anywhere. You could be . . . gazing at one of . . . Christo's umbrellas . . . just enjoying art for art's sake. Maybe discussing it with a loved one. "I think there's a significant ba—" THUNK! "Honey . . . there seems to be an umbrella imbedded in my chest."

You must accelerate. Lust. Laugh. Live every day as if it's your last. Go shopping. Buy whatever you want. A Ming vase. Chocolate furniture. The bones of Elvis Presley. Go ahead. Load up your credit cards. Shoot a cop. Fuck a stranger. Fuck him, kill him, eat him. Fly to Rome and give the finger to the Pope. Enjoy.

During World War II, an American soldier was held in a Japanese POW camp. Locked in a cell without windows for three years. No sunlight. No exercise. No human contact. No books. Just bread and water. Every day, for one thousand one hundred and ninety-five days. You know how he survived? Not by religion. Not by plotting his revenge.

Eggs.

This man loved eggs. He adored them. So every day he would think about eggs. Every night he would dream about eggs. Scrambled eggs. Poached eggs. Eggs over easy. Fried, boiled, jumbo brown. Eggs with bacon, eggs with toast, eggs with other eggs. When the war was over, he rejoiced. He flew home to Kansas. He met his parents. They drove him to the local diner where all his family and friends welcomed him back. Then he sat down and ordered breakfast. He ate a twelve-egg omelet. He ate it quickly. He enjoyed every last bite. And then–he had a massive heart attack and dropped dead on the floor.

Now some people think this story shows just how cruel fate can be. How sad. I disagree. I think it shows just how miraculous life really is. That man was never again going to be as happy as he was in that split second after he'd swallowed his last bite of eggs and pushed the plate aside. He got what he wanted. Imagine how good that omelet must have tasted to him. No matter what he did for the rest of his life, it would never add up to that moment in the diner. Marilyn Monroe could have jetted to Kansas and fucked him silly, and when you asked him how it was, he would've said, "Well, it wasn't the eggs."

Most people think life sucks, and then you die. Not me. I beg to differ. I think life sucks, then you get cancer, then your dog dies, your wife leaves you, the cancer goes into remission, you get a new dog, you get remarried, you owe ten million dollars in medical bills but you work hard for thirty-five years and you pay it back and then— one day—you have a massive stroke, your whole right side is paralyzed, you have to limp along the streets and speak out of the left side of your mouth and drool but you go into rehabilitation and regain the power to walk and the power to talk and then—one day—you step off a curb at Sixty-seventh Street, and BANG you get hit by a city bus and then you die. Maybe.

I think Jim Henson said it best when he said, "Anybody got some aspirin? I think I've got a cold."

And a chill filled the room.

We all have this incredible attachment to the Muppets, don't we?

"We love the Muppets. They're so cute."

Because of that, we miss the point of Jim Henson's life

and his death. If his life and death teach you anything, it should be this: enjoy it while you're here, because when you are gone you have lost all control.

Did you hear about Jim Henson's funeral here in New York City?

Big Bird and Kermit the Frog sang "It's Not Easy Being Green" at Jim Henson's funeral.

If I'm fifty-six years old when I kick the bucket and a sock is singing at my funeral, I'm going to pop right out of the coffin and go, "What is this? Sammy Davis, Jr., gets Frank Sinatra and I get a fucking sock? I'm pissed off now. I am definitely coming back to haunt you people."

(The stage lights fade slowly as the murky guitar chords merge into a loud dirgelike rhythm. The stage is now bathed in soft blue light as the guitar player saunters on from the shadows.)

We've spent a lot of time tonight talking about death and disease and cancer and catastrophe. We do it almost every night. And we do it because . . . well, because I think it's funny.

But I want to send you home on an upbeat note. With a message. With a dance number. A toe-tapper. A number that puts a smile on your face and a nice warm feeling down deep in the cockles of your heart.

(Singing)

Everything is horrible.
Yeah.
Really really terrible.
Uh-huh.
I'm really depressed,

I'm really downtrodden.
Yeah.
The whole world is doomed.
We're all gonna die.
25,672 people die every single minute.
Uh-huh.
Oh yeah.
Yeah, yeah.
Seventeen hundred and fifty people just died.
Cancer, death, AIDS, inflation, period.
Taxes, George Bush.
Hell.
Satan.
Cancer of the face, cancer of the colon.
Cancer of the wrist.
And John Denver on compact disk.
Oh, no.
No no.

(The stage goes dark. A single spotlight hits the guitar player as he flails away at his instrument. Slowly the lights fade up. Denis stubs out his cigarette and lights a new one. He steps to the front of the stage.)

(Spoken)

17,675 more people just fucking died.
Remember that woman who went to the ladies' room?
She's dead now.
You'll never see her again.
Kind of sad, isn't it?
Because you never asked her name.
You thought she was just a person sitting next to you in a theatre.

Now she's dead.
Now she's gone.

(Singing)

JFK, RFK, LBJ, FDR.
Drive, he said.
Uh-huh.
Oh yeah.
Malcolm X.
Lenny Bruce.
The little chick from the *Poltergeist* movies.
Uh-huh.
Oh yeah.
Uh-huh.
Miles Davis.
Redd Foxx.
Stan Getz.
Joe Papp.
Strike the pose.
Strike the pose.
Uh-huh.
Oh no.
Oh no no no.
Michael Landon.
Oh no.
Freddie Mercury.
Oh no.
Fred MacMurray.
Oh no no no.

(Spoken)

I've got this pain in my left arm that goes all the way
from my shoulder to my thumb. I've had this tightness in

my chest for a couple of weeks now. It's a Pete Maravich kind of thing. I've been worried about it for a couple of days now. I—ungh—(*Clutches chest. Gasps. Music comes to an abrupt stop.*)

Just kidding, folks. You didn't really think that I—ungh—ach—

(*Clutches chest. Gasps. Collapses dead onto the stage. The music stops. The guitar player glances down at Denis. He taps the body with his foot.*)

Denis? Denis?

(*He leans down. Checks for a pulse. The wrist. The neck. Nothing. He pries the burning cigarette from between Denis's rigid fingers. He stands up. He inhales. He smiles. He exhales.*)

Ahhh.

(*Waving happily to audience*)

Good night, everybody!

(*BLACK OUT. Iggy Pop's "Lust for Life" blares loudly into the house for three and a half minutes and then fades.*)

ABOUT THE AUTHOR

Denis Leary taught for five years at Emerson College in Boston where he cofounded and directed the Comedy Workshop. Before its Off Broadway production, *No Cure for Cancer* won the Critics Award at the Edinburgh International Arts Festival. Leary's writing has appeared in *Ploughshares, The Colorado Review, New Musical Express* and other publications. A native of Worcester, Massachusetts, he lives in New York City.